MUSICAL REFERENCES
AND SONG TEXTS IN THE BIBLE

Geary Larrick

Studies in the History and Interpretation of Music
Volume 9

The Edwin Mellen Press
Lewiston/Queenston/Lampeter

Library of Congress Cataloging in Publication Data

This volume has been registered with The Library of Congress.

This is volume 9 in the continuing series
Studies in the History and Interpretation of Music
Volume 9 ISBN 0-88946-492-8
SHIM Series ISBN 0-88946-426-X

A CIP catalog record for this book
is available from the British Library.

The Edwin Mellen Press   The Edwin Mellen Press
        Box 450   Box 67
    Lewiston, N.Y.   Queenston, Ontario
     USA 14092   CANADA L0S 1L0

                    Edwin Mellen Press, Ltd
                    Lampeter, Dyfed, Wales,
                  UNITED KINGDOM SA48 7DY

            Printed in the United States of America

DEDICATION

To my parents:

Clyde Henderson Larrick (1907-78)

Gail Geary Larrick (1907-79)

ACKNOWLEDGEMENT

Artworks in this volume were drawn by
Professor Herbert Sandmann, Stevens Point, Wisconsin,
and are used with permission of the artist.

CONTENTS

Preface

viii

Section I: Musical References in the Bible
Essay: On Various Editions of the Bible 1
Foreword to Section I 5
Alphabetical Listing by Musical Term:
bell(s) 9
cornet(s) 10
cymbal(s) 13
dulcimer 17
flute 19
harp(s) 22
harped, harpers 27
harping 27
hymn(s) 29
instrument(s) 31
instrument of ten strings 36
melody 38
musical 39
Musician 40
musicians 43
musick 44
organ(s) 48
pipe(s) 50
piped 51
pipers 51
Psalm 52
psalm 56
psalmist, Psalms 56
psalms 56
psaltery(ies) 59
ram's horn, rams' horns 63
sackbut 65
sang 66
sing 68
singer(s) 75
singeth, singing 78
song 82
songs 87
spiritual songs 89
sung 89
tabret(s) 92
timbrel(s) 95
trumpet(s) 98
trumpeters 107
viol(s) 109

Section II: Song Texts in the Bible
Foreword to Section II 111
Essay: On the Definition of Song 112
Listing of Song Texts:
Song of Moses 114
Song of Miriam 115
Three Poetic Fragments
From the Book of Numbers 115
Song of the Well 115
Taunt Song 116
Song, or Psalm, of Moses 117
Song of Deborah 121
Song of Hannah 124
Elegy for Saul and Jonathan 125
Hymn of Praise 126
Hymn 130
Song of Victory 131
Song of Apocalypse 132
Song of Thanksgiving 133
Canticle 134
Magnificat 135
Benedictus 136
From the Book of Luke 137
Two Excerpts from the Book of Revelation 138
Song of Solomon 139

Afterword   147

Bibliography   148

Index   151

PREFACE

The Holy Bible contains many references to music and to musical instruments. The primary purpose of this volume is to list these references in their entirety, with some commentary added. Scriptural references are taken, for the most part, from the English language King James Version, or Authorized Version, which was first published in 1611 A.D.

This book is divided into two main sections, with an essay and foreword at the beginning of each section. The original artworks are artistic, rather than descriptive in nature, and help elucidate the beauty of music as perceived by this author. Section I is comprised of an alphabetical listing of musical terms accompanied by the singular verse in which each term appears in the Bible, while Section II contains song texts that have been found in the holy Scriptures. The 150 psalms have not been included separately, although it is understood that the book of Psalms in the Holy Bible is a type of hymn-book by itself, without notated music. The Psalms were originally sung, and often are set to music in the 20th Century.

Organization and content of this volume on music and the Bible have been planned with two types of readers in mind--those who wish to use the book as a reference, and those who prefer to read it from cover to cover. The bibliography offers the reader further sources, many of which have influenced this particular book.

Section I
Musical References in the Bible

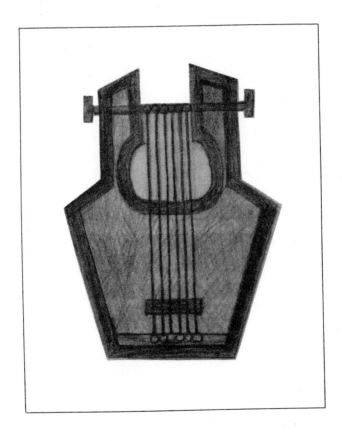

Essay: On Various Editions of the Bible

There have been several, if not many, editions of the holy Scriptures over the centuries. The advent of printing with movable type in 15th-Century Europe and the Far East has brought about an explosion of shared verbiage among cultures and peoples up to the present time. A most respected English language edition of the 17th Century was the Authorized Version, also called the King James Version. This edition was first published in 1611 in England, and has been reprinted in several editions in the 20th Century.

Other English language editions of the 20th Century include the Revised Standard Version, the Jerusalem Bible, and the New English Bible. Early Biblical manuscripts were in Hebrew, Greek and Latin. In latter 20th Century America, there are several English language editions of the Scriptures in existence.

Following are a few specific comparisons among three editions in regard to musical references. The three editions chosen are the King James Version, the Revised Standard Version, and the New English Bible. Abbreviations used in the following comparisons are "KJV," "RSV," and "NEB," respectively.[1]

Genesis 4:21 ----

    KJV - instruments mentioned are harp and pipe

    RSV - instruments mentioned are lyre and pipe

    NEB - instruments mentioned are harp and pipe

I Samuel 10:5 ----

    KJV - instruments mentioned are psaltery, tabret, pipe and harp

    RSV - instruments mentioned are harp, tambourine, flute and lyre

    NEB - instruments mentioned are lute, harp, fife and drum

---

[1]The following RSV Bible text is from the Revised Standard Version Bible, copyright 1946, 1952, 1971 by the Division of Christian Education of the National Council of the Churches of Christ in the U.S.A., and is used by permission. The following NEB text is taken from The New English Bible, copyright by The Delegates of Oxford University Press and The Syndics of the Cambridge University Press, 1961, 1970; reprinted with permission.

II Chronicles 29:27 ----

"instruments" and "trumpets" are mentioned identically in KJV, RSV, and NEB

Job 21:12 ----

KJV - instruments mentioned are the timbrel, harp and organ

RSV - instruments mentioned are tambourine, lyre and pipe

NEB - instruments mentioned are tambourine, harp and flute

Psalm 150:4 ----

KJV - artistic terms mentioned are timbrel, dance, stringed instruments, organs

RSV - artistic terms mentioned are timbrel, dance, strings, pipe

NEB - artistic terms mentioned include tambourines, dancing, flute, strings

Daniel 3:5 ----

KJV - musical terms mentioned are cornet, flute, harp, sackbut, psaltery, dulcimer and musick

RSV - musical terms mentioned are horn, pipe, lyre, trigon, harp, bagpipe and music

NEB - musical terms mentioned are horn, pipe, zither, triangle, dulcimer, music and singing

I Corinthians 13:1 ----

KJV - musical terms mentioned are "sounding brass" and "tinkling cymbal"

RSV - musical terms mentioned are "noisy gong" and "clanging cymbal"

NEB - musical terms mentioned are "sounding gong" and "clanging cymbal"

Revelation 18:22 ----

KJV - musical terms mentioned are harpers, musicians, pipers, trumpeters

RSV - musical terms mentioned are harpers, minstrels, flute players, trumpeters

NEB - musical terms mentioned are harpers, minstrels, flute-players, trumpeters

In conclusion, there are slight deviations among the various editions of the Bible, as represented by the foregoing comparisons. Since the topics here discussed are musical terms and references, the reader should have minimal problems in interpreting religious meaning from the Scriptures based upon specific differences which presumably appear from edition to edition. The reader who is searching the Scriptures for moral guidance or history of civilization might not be overly concerned with whether the original author(s), long since passed on, actually mentioned the equivalent of a zither or a dulcimer, for example.

The student of modern musical instruments knows that in the latter 20th Century there are in existence many, many musical instruments throughout the world: the relatively new field of ethnomusicology is presently beginning to document some of these instruments and their uses. Of the numerous musical instruments in existence, some are documented by photograph, some by literal description and others by audio recording. The list of musical instruments in the late 20th Century is practically endless, and there is no reason to suspect that this has not been true throughout recorded history of civilization. Although the modern communication student/scholar might disagree in viewpoint, the musician tends to regard language and depiction as only a means to an end, not the end itself. In regard to musical references in the Bible, the actual music that existed is the musician's end, while contemporary description is the musician's secondary record. The musician tends to look at depiction in elusive, musical terms that can be described only in an artistic, not literal, fashion. Thus, for example, the literal depiction in the Bible of a zither or dulcimer is not so important regarding detail, to the musician, as it is regarding relativity. In other words, the modern reader is guided to notice the relative difference between a Biblical "zither" and "dulcimer," but not to be bothered so much by exact definition of these musical instruments, since the original Scriptural manuscript lies centuries in the past. This editor/author suggests that the reader might "look" into the Scriptures with both a realistic and a philosophical eye, because of the many translations and editions handed down through the centuries: many, many legitimate messages are contained in the Scriptures, and it is the reader's task to interpret and to determine the specifics of those messages as they apply to his or her life, perhaps with the assistance and fellowship of other interested persons.

Foreword to Section I

The following list of quotations from the Holy Bible is ordered alphabetically, according to the specific musical term that is mentioned in the Scriptures. Each term is discussed briefly prior to its listing, with the editor gathering from various references listed in the Bibliography near the end of this volume, as well as from his collected knowledge as a professional musician and educator.

A problem of names arises because of our lack of direct knowledge, as well as the language difficulties associated with the Bible having been translated several times. The Holy Bible has been handed down by many people over the span of several centuries culminating, in this instance, with the King James Version of 17th-Century England. The Shakespearean dialect of this particular edition includes various words known to people of that time which might not be familiar to the contemporary reader. This type of reading problem is apparent in all literature, however, whether it is technical, popular or religious in nature. In the following section, terms like "psaltery," "dulcimer," "cornet," "trumpet," "pipe," "flute" and "sackbut" lend a 17th-Century European flavor to Scriptures that were originally composed several centuries previously in another part of the world.

The numerous musical instruments that are mentioned in the Holy Bible can be grouped into five classes, namely:
  a) the human voice
  b) keyboard instrument(s)
  c) stringed instruments
  d) wind instruments
  e) percussion instruments

Significantly, in the latter 20th Century have been added only the electronic musical instruments to those five basic classes included in the Bible. The human voice as a musical instrument, involving words like "sing" and "singer" in the following section, is of course a primary vehicle for musical expression in the 20th Century, as it obviously was during the era described in the Holy Bible. The only keyboard instrument listed in Section I is the organ, for the piano was not invented until the period known as the Baroque in

Western music history. Likewise, the keyboard percussion sub-class known as the xylophone is not mentioned in the Bible, although it is probable that a xylophone-type instrument did exist at that time in other parts of the world.

Stringed instruments mentioned in the Bible include the viol, harp and psaltery. Presumably the viol would have been played by drawing a bow across strings, while the harp and psaltery would have been plucked with the fingers or with a small object held by the fingers, called a plectrum. The dulcimer might have been struck with mallets in a percussive fashion.

Wind instruments mentioned in the Holy Bible include the ram's horn, the cornet and the trumpet. It is interesting to speculate the difference between the Biblical cornets and trumpets: was it comparable with 20th-Century brass-wind instruments? Or perhaps there was some other kind of equivalent difference between the two instruments, which further scholarship can reveal. The only woodwind instruments mentioned in Section I are the flute and pipe, although various reed-vibrated musical instruments are known to have existed in ancient Greece.

Percussion musical instruments mentioned in the Bible include the tabret, which was presumably a small drum played with the hands and fingers, as well as bells and cymbals. Biblical cymbals probably were of various sizes, and the bells would have been suspended in various methods and numbers. The percussive timbrel was apparently similar to our present-day tambourine, which is a small frame drum with jingles.

In the following section, this editor has chosen to repeat Biblical verses without constraint, where duplications appear in the Scriptures. Thus a single verse might have several musical references: that verse is written in Section I accompanying each of the musical terms and may therefore appear several times throughout the entire section. For example, the Biblical book of Daniel, chapter 3, verse 10 (abbreviated Daniel 3:10) contains several musical references--cornet, flute, harp, sackbut, psaltery, dulcimer and musick--in the King James Version. This particular verse is then listed after each of those seven terms, which are catalogued alphabetically. It is hoped that the following listing will prove to be elucidative for the reader, as well as enjoyable to peruse.

ALPHABETICAL LISTING BY MUSICAL TERM

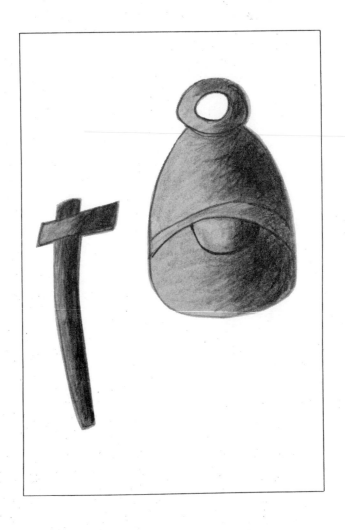

bell(s)

The bell is a metallic percussion instrument that is sounded by striking with a beater. If the beater is installed permanently in the bell, as in church bells and cow bells, the beater is called a clapper. Bells of the 20th Century range in size from small bells suspended on ropes in India, to the huge church steeple bells of Europe, North America and other continents. Cup bells of various sizes are used in Japanese music, often struck with a rubber-covered beater or mallet; these bells are also used in meditation and worship practice. Unlike the previously mentioned bells, the orchestral bells of the modern symphony orchestra are tuned to specific pitches similarly to the piano. A similar instrument, the glockenspiel, is also used in a considerable amount of modern music. The characteristic sound of a bell usually involves a metallic timbre, or tone color, as well as a resonance of quite long duration. One might assume that the bells of the holy Scriptures were not tuned to specific pitches, and perhaps were not arranged or organized by the performers to allow for an intended sequence of sounds, although this is possible. Obviously "bells of gold" were chosen for visual beauty and adorned for decoration, in addition to their aural qualities.

Exodus 28:33 - And beneath upon the hem of it thou shalt make pomegranates of blue, and of purple, and of scarlet, round about the hem thereof; and bells of gold between them round about:

Exodus 28:34 - A golden bell and a pomegranate, a golden bell and a pomegranate, upon the hem of the robe round about.

Exodus 39:25 - And they made bells of pure gold, and put the bells between the pomegranates upon the hem of the robe, round about between the pomegranates;

Exodus 39:26 - A bell and a pomegranate, a bell and a pomegranate, round about the hem of the robe to minister in; as the Lord commanded Moses.

Zechariah 14:20 - In that day shall there be upon the bells of the horses, HOLINESS UNTO THE LORD; and the pots in the Lord's house shall be like the bowls before the altar.

cornet(s)

Performers of the brasswind musical instruments could discuss interminably the possible differences between the trumpet and the cornet as they are mentioned in the Holy Bible, King James Version. The contemporary cornet has been around only since the 19th Century, and is used sparingly in the modern symphony orchestra. The 20th-Century cornet has three valves which are pushed by the performer's fingers to effect changes in pitch production, and is known for its "sweet" sound, in contrast to the more "heraldic" sound of the contemporary trumpet. In much educational music today in the United States of America, the cornet is used interchangeably with the trumpet, although their actual timbres are not identical. The brass bands of contemporary England and the United States, that is, wind bands without woodwind instruments, use several cornet- and trumpet-types with valves. The drum and bugle corps of the late 20th Century also use several similar instruments with and without valves.

The European Renaissance cornett was made of wood or ivory with a cup-shaped mouthpiece, in contrast to the 20th-Century cornet made of metal with a cup-shaped mouthpiece. In Biblical references, "cornet" and "trumpet" are sometimes used exclusively; however, occasionally they appear within the same passage. It is this editor/author's opinion that early Biblical scholars perceived a difference linguistically between what we now read as "cornet" and "trumpet," although the details of that difference remain a mystery at this time.

II Samuel 6:5 - And David and all the house of Israel played before the Lord on all manner of instruments made of fir wood, even on harps, and on psalteries, and on timbrels, and on cornets, and on cymbals.

I Chronicles 15:28 - Thus all Israel brought up the ark of the covenant of the Lord with shouting, and with sound of the cornet, and with trumpets, and with cymbals, making a noise with psalteries and harps.

II Chronicles 15:14 - And they sware unto the Lord with a loud voice, and with shouting, and with trumpets, and with cornets.

Psalm 98:6 - With trumpets and sound of cornet make a joyful noise before the Lord, the King.

Daniel 3:5 - That at what time ye hear the sound of the <u>cornet</u>, flute, harp, sackbut, psaltery, dulcimer,and all kinds of musick, ye fall down and worship the golden image that Nebuchadnezzar the king hath set up:

Daniel 3:7 - Therefore at that time, when all the people heard the sound of the <u>cornet</u>, flute, harp, sackbut, psaltery, and all kinds of musick, all the people, the nations, and the languages, fell down and worshipped the golden image that Nebuchadnezzar the king had set up.

Daniel 3:10 - Thou, O king, hast made a decree, that every man that shall hear the sound of the <u>cornet</u>, flute, harp, sackbut, psaltery, and dulcimer, and all kinds of musick, shall fall down and worship the golden image:

Daniel 3:15 - Now if ye be ready that at what time ye hear the sound of the <u>cornet</u>, flute, harp, sackbut, psaltery, and dulcimer, and all kinds of musick, ye fall down and worship the image which I have made; well: but if ye worship not, ye shall be cast the same hour into the midst of a burning fiery furnace; and who is that God that shall deliver you out of my hands?

Hosea 5:8 - Blow ye the <u>cornet</u> in Gibeah, and the trumpet in Ramah: cry aloud at Beth-aven, after thee, O Benjamin.

cymbal(s)

It might seem incongruent to the present-day connoisseur of music that the same instrument can be used in symphonic music of Peter Tchaikovsky as well as in "heavy metal" popular music, yet can be associated with exaltation within the holy Scriptures: this is the case with the percussive cymbals. The cymbal of the 20th Century is made of a mixture of brass and other ingredients. It is available in many sizes, thicknesses and weights, resulting in a veritable palette of timbres. There is reason to suspect that several contrasts in tone colors were available to cymbalists of Biblical times, based on the various placements of the term within the Holy Bible. Cymbals today, as then, can be clashed together, or suspended singularly and struck with a mallet, stick or beater. The latter technique, though not often associated with Scriptural references, is suggested in the New Testament verse in First Corinthians which refers to a "tinkling" cymbal. Presumably the cymbals of the Scriptures were not of definite pitch, as are the small tuned "antique" cymbals requested by some modern composers (for example, Claude Debussy), but were primarily metallic noise makers. Their Scriptural listings with instruments like the harp and psaltery lead one to conclude that the cymbals of Biblical times were not always played loudly.

It should be kept in mind that the Bible describes life in the part of the world known today as the Middle East, an area that ideologically is between the traditional cymbal musics of the Western world and those of eastern Asia. The metallic cymbal has been traditionally an integral part of meditative music in eastern Asia, and has produced a myriad of musical colors through the centuries in China, Japan, Indonesia and elsewhere. In the Western world by contrast, the cymbal has apparently not always been an important part of worship music through the centuries, often having the reputation of being rather crude aesthetically. In this light, the cymbal references contained in the Holy Bible should be quite revealing to the modern Western church participant who perhaps has never heard a beautiful noise made by a cymbal associated with worship!

14

II Samuel 6:5 - And David and all the house of Israel played before the Lord on all manner of instruments made of fir wood, even on harps, and on psalteries, and on timbrels, and on cornets, and on cymbals.

I Chronicles 13:8 - And David and all Israel played before God with all their might, and with singing, and with harps, and with psalteries, and with timbrels, and with cymbals, and with trumpets.

I Chronicles 15:16 - And David spake to the chief of the Levites to appoint their brethren to be the singers with instruments of musick, psalteries and harps and cymbals, sounding, by lifting up the voice with joy.

I Chronicles 15:19 - So the singers, Heman, Asaph, and Ethan, were appointed to sound with cymbals of brass;

I Chronicles 15:28 - Thus all Israel brought up the ark of the covenant of the Lord with shouting, and with sound of the cornet, and with trumpets, and with cymbals, making a noise with psalteries and harps.

I Chronicles 16:5 - Asaph the chief, and next to him Zechariah, Jeiel, and Shemiramoth, and Jehiel, and Mattithiah, and Eliab, and Benaiah, and Obed-edom: and Jeiel with psalteries and with harps; but Asaph made a sound with cymbals;

I Chronicles 16:42 - And with them Heman and Jeduthun with trumpets and cymbals for those that should make a sound, and with musical instruments of God. And the sons of Jeduthun were porters.

I Chronicles 25:1 - Moreover David and the captains of the host separated to the service of the sons of Asaph, and of Heman, and of Jeduthun, who should prophesy with harps, with psalteries, and with cymbals: and the number of the workmen according to their service was:

I Chronicles 25:6 - All these were under the hands of their father for song in the house of the Lord, with cymbals, psalteries, and harps, for the service of the house of God, according to the king's order to Asaph, Jeduthun, and Heman.

II Chronicles 5:12 - Also the Levites which were the singers, all of them of Asaph, of Heman, of Jeduthun, with their sons and their brethren, being arrayed in white linen, having cymbals and psalteries and harps, stood at the east end of the altar, and with them an hundred and twenty priests sounding with trumpets:

II Chronicles 5:13 - It came even to pass, as the trumpeters and singers were as one, to make one sound to be heard in praising and thanking the Lord; and when they lifted up their voice with the trumpets and cymbals and instruments of musick, and praised the Lord, saying, For he is good; for his mercy endureth for ever: that then the house was filled with a cloud, even the house of the Lord;

II Chronicles 29:25 - And he set the Levites in the house of the Lord with cymbals, with psalteries, and with harps, according to the commandment of David, and of Gad the king's seer, and Nathan the prophet: for so was the commandment of the Lord by his prophets.

Ezra 3:10 - And when the builders laid the foundation of the temple of the Lord, they set the priests in their apparel with trumpets, and the Levites the sons of Asaph with cymbals, to praise the Lord, after the ordinance of David king of Israel.

Nehemiah 12:27 - And at the dedication of the wall of Jerusalem they sought the Levites out of all their places, to bring them to Jerusalem, to keep the dedication with gladness, both with the thanksgivings, and with singing, with cymbals, psalteries, and with harps.

Psalm 150:5 - Praise him upon the loud cymbals: praise him upon the high sounding cymbals.

I Corinthians 13:1 - Though I speak with the tongues of men and of angels, and have not charity, I am become as sounding brass, or a tinkling cymbal.

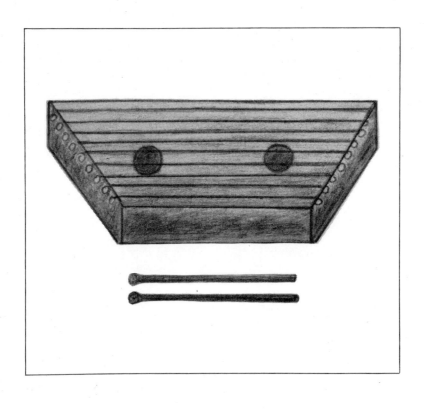

dulcimer

As one learns the history of many musical instruments, one finds that a given instrument changes from time to time and from place to place. So it is with the dulcimer. The dulcimer can be linked with similar instruments such as the psaltery, zither, cimbalom and pantaleon. The instrument and its type have appeared in several parts of the world through the ages, including China, Europe, and North America. The accepted description presently is a soundboard with several tightly stretched strings that are struck by the performer with mallets or "hammers." Indeed, the hammered dulcimer can be found in the latter 20th Century in folk-music situations, often in the mountains as well as in the cities. As a European mediaeval instrument, the dulcimer eventually developed into the harpsichord and pianoforte when mechanical action and a keyboard to be played by the fingers were added.

Daniel 3:5 - That at what time ye hear the sound of the cornet, flute, harp, sackbut, psaltery, dulcimer, and all kinds of musick, ye fall down and worship the golden image that Nebuchadnezzar the king hath set up:

Daniel 3:10 - Thou, O king, hast made a decree, that every man that shall hear the sound of the cornet, flute, harp, sackbut, psaltery, and dulcimer, and all kinds of musick, shall fall down and worship the golden image:

Daniel 3:15 - Now if ye be ready that at what time ye hear the sound of the cornet, flute, harp, sackbut, psaltery, and dulcimer, and all kinds of musick, ye fall down and worship the image which I have made; well: but if ye worship not, ye shall be cast the same hour into the midst of a burning fiery furnace; and who is that God that shall deliver you out of my hands?

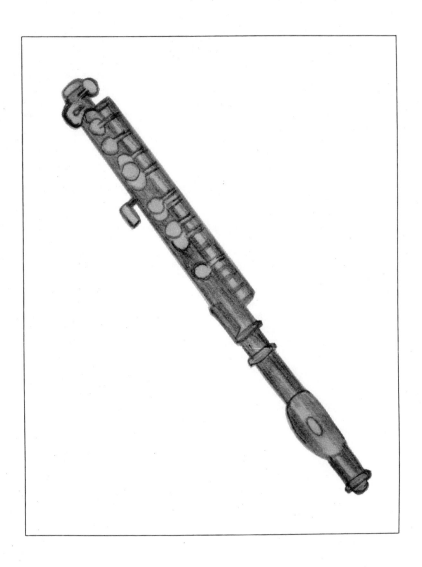

flute

The flute of course is recognized as one of the most beautiful sounding of musical instruments, and it has been around practically from the beginning of recorded history. Early flutes were made of clay and hollowed-out stalks of bamboo, as well as other materials. Throughout the world today, simple "homemade" flutes are plentiful in many cultures, often with six finger holes. The fipple flute, or recorder, of the European Renaissance and early Baroque was a participant in much excellent musical literature, culminating in the sonatas of Telemann and Handel before being replaced in the growing symphony orchestra by the transverse flute as we know it. The six-hole flute and recorder are still present today around the world: the six-hole flute is especially popular among Indian and Chinese peoples, and the recorder is used as an educational instrument in England and the United States of America currently. It is questionable if new inventions of plastic applied to making recorders are actually an improvement over the wooden instruments of the past, in regard to the qualitative sound produced.

During the 19th Century the German instrument maker Theobold Boehm made various technological improvements on the flute of that era to help produce the instrument commonly played today in bands, orchestras and chamber music. The 20th-Century flute is a metallic tube with several finger holes and keys, made sometimes with silver, platinum or gold.

Generically the flute includes an entire family of instruments of various sizes and sounding ranges, including the piccolo--which has a very high-pitched, sometimes shrill sound, and the bass flute--which has a considerably more mellow, low-pitched sound. The extended family of flutes would include the military fife as well as the pipe that is mentioned in the Bible and was popular in mediaeval and Renaissance Europe.

Daniel 3:5 - That at what time ye hear the sound of the cornet, flute, harp, sackbut, psaltery, dulcimer, and all kinds of musick, ye fall down and worship the golden image that Nebuchadnezzar the king hath set up:

Daniel 3:7 - Therefore at that time, when all the people heard the sound of the cornet, flute, harp, sackbut, psaltery, and all kinds of musick, all the people, the nations, and the languages, fell down and worshipped the golden image that Nebuchadnezzar the king had set up.

Daniel 3:10 - Thou, O king, hast made a decree, that every man that shall hear the sound of the cornet, flute, harp, sackbut, psaltery, and dulcimer, and all kinds of musick, shall fall down and worship the golden image:

Daniel 3:15 - Now if ye be ready that at what time ye hear the sound of the cornet, flute, harp, sackbut, psaltery, and dulcimer, and all kinds of musick, ye fall down and worship the image which I have made; well: but if ye worship not, ye shall be cast the same hour into the midst of a burning fiery furnace; and who is that God that shall deliver you out of my hands?

harp(s)

The beautiful-sounding harp has been in existence at least since 3000 B.C. in Mesopotamia. Contemporary music students study about the kithara, an instrument that was present in ancient Greece. It is not certain whether Jews of the Biblical era had the harp as we know it, or the lyre. The King James edition of the Bible does not contain the word "lyre," and thus the word "harp" is probably used generically throughout the Bible to identify a plucked string instrument. David's proficiency on the harp is variously documented throughout the Scriptures, and undoubtedly stimulated many art works depicting the lyre and harp in the Middle Ages and Renaissance. As such, the harp is associated with things celestial, and some people must surely not be surprised if David himself greets them at Heaven's gates playing the harp!

As with the wind instruments, the harp was mechanically "improved" during the 19th Century, and was introduced as an adjunct member of the symphony orchestra. The contemporary concert harp has pedals and a considerably wide pitch range, and is often enjoyed in the performance of music by Tchaikovsky and others. Ballet music of the 19th Century seems to have a particularly successful use of the concert harp, as does orchestral music of Maurice Ravel. European mediaeval music employs the smaller harp very effectively, although before 1600 much Western classical music was generic rather than idiomatic; that is, the music was composed and notated for no specific instrumentation at times, or for various options. A keyboard part might be performed on the harp, and vice versa, for example. Thus in modern performances of those musics, considerable decision-making is done by the performers themselves, sometimes more successfully than at other times, from the standpoint of the audience.

For a person of the 20th Century to undertake study of the concert harp, considerable investment is required. The modern harp is quite expensive, and not at all easy to learn to play well. For those willing to commit the required energy, discipline and finances, however, there awaits the opportunity to produce absolutely exquisite musical sounds on a rather rare instrument. There are a few harpists usually near or in major cities, and there exist harp societies and conventions at least on the national, if not the international, level. Major orchestras hire the harpist full-time as other personnel, while orchestras with smaller budgets hire the harpist per rehearsal or concert. Unlike the violin, much orchestral literature does not include the harp, although when the harpist does perform within a symphony orchestra, he or she often is faced with music exposed in a soloistic manner. Thus the harp in an orchestra is decidedly in a minority position, perhaps at a ratio of 1:100, but this fact does not take away from the importance of the instrument within the ensemble.

Such is not the case with harp references in the Holy Bible. The harp is mentioned in many situations, even in such words as "harping" and "harped." It is small wonder that the harp has been associated with rejoicing and with angelic beings, based on the wealth of associations connected with the instrument in the Scriptures.

Genesis 4:21 - And his brother's name was Jubal: he was the father of all such as handle the harp and organ.

Genesis 31:27 - Wherefore didst thou flee away secretly, and steal away from me; and didst not tell me, that I might have sent thee away with mirth, and with songs, with tabret, and with harp?

I Samuel 10:5 - After that thou shalt come to the hill of God, where is the garrison of the Philistines: and it shall come to pass, when thou art come thither to the city, that thou shalt meet a company of prophets coming down from the high place with a psaltery, and a tabret, and a pipe, and a harp, before them; and they shall prophesy:

I Samuel 16:16 - Let our lord now command thy servants, which are before thee, to seek out a man, who is a cunning player on an harp: and it shall come to pass, when the evil spirit from God is upon thee, that he shall play with his hand, and thou shalt be well.

I Samuel 16:23 - And it came to pass, when the evil spirit from God was upon Saul, that David took an harp, and played with his hand: so Saul was refreshed, and was well, and the evil spirit departed from him.

II Samuel 6:5 - And David and all the house of Israel played before the Lord on all manner of instruments made of fir wood, even on harps, and on psalteries, and on timbrels, and on cornets, and on cymbals.

I Kings 10:12 - And the king made of the almug trees pillars for the house of the Lord, and for the king's house, harps also and psalteries for singers: there came no such almug trees, nor were seen unto this day.

I Chronicles 13:8 - And David and all Israel played before God with all their might, and with singing, and with harps,and with psalteries, and with timbrels, and with cymbals, and with trumpets.

I Chronicles 15:16 - And David spake to the chief of the Levites to appoint their brethren to be the singers with instruments of musick, psalteries and harps and cymbals, sounding, by lifting up the voice with joy.

I Chronicles 15:21 - And Mattithiah, and Elipheleh, and Mikneiah, and Obededom, and Jeiel, and Azaziah, with harps on the Sheminith to excel.

I Chronicles 15:28 - Thus all Israel brought up the ark of the covenant of the Lord with shouting, and with sound of the cornet, and with trumpets, and with cymbals, making a noise with psalteries and harps.

I Chronicles 16:5 - Asaph the chief, and next to him Zechariah, Jeiel, and Shemiramoth, and Jehiel, and Mattithiah, and Eliab, and Benaiah, and Obed-edom: and Jeiel with psalteries and with harps; but Asaph made a sound with cymbals;

I Chronicles 25:1 - Moreover David and the captains of the host separated to the service of the sons of Asaph, and of Heman, and of Jeduthun, who should prophesy with harps, with psalteries, and with cymbals: and the number of the workmen according to their service was:

I Chronicles 25:3 - Of Jeduthun: the songs of Jeduthun; Gedaliah, and Zeri, and Jeshaiah, Hashabiah, and Mattithiah, six, under the hands of their father Jeduthun, who prophesied with a harp, to give thanks and to praise the Lord.

I Chronicles 25:6 - All these were under the hands of their father for song in the house of the Lord, with cymbals, psalteries, and harps, for the service of the house of God, according to the king's order to Asaph, Jeduthun, and Heman.

II Chronicles 5:12 - Also the Levites which were the singers, all of them of Asaph, of Heman, of Jeduthun, with their sons and their brethren, being arrayed in white linen, having cymbals and psalteries and harps, stood at the east end of the altar, and with them an hundred and twenty priests sounding with trumpets:)

II Chronicles 9:11 - And the king made of the algum trees terraces to the house of the Lord, and to the king's palace, and harps and psalteries for singers: and there were none such seen before in the land of Judah.

II Chronicles 20:28 - And they came to Jerusalem with psalteries and harps and trumpets unto the house of the Lord.

II Chronicles 29:25 - And he set the Levites in the house of the Lord with cymbals, with psalteries, and with <u>harps</u>, according to the commandment of David, and of Gad the king's seer, and Nathan the prophet: for so was the commandment of the Lord by his prophets.

Nehemiah 12:27 - And at the dedication of the wall of Jerusalem they sought the Levites out of all their places, to bring them to Jerusalem, to keep the dedication with gladness, both with the thanksgivings, and with singing, with cymbals, psalteries, and with <u>harps</u>.

Job 21:12 - They take the timbrel and <u>harp</u>, and rejoice at the sound of the organ.

Job 30:31 - My <u>harp</u> also is turned to mourning, and my organ into the voice of them that weep.

Psalm 33:2 - Praise the Lord with <u>harp</u>: sing unto him with the psaltery and an instrument of ten strings.

Psalm 43:4 - Then I will go unto the altar of God, unto God my exceeding joy: yea, upon the <u>harp</u> will I praise thee, O God my God.

Psalm 49:4 - I will incline mine ear to a parable: I will open my dark saying upon the <u>harp</u>.

Psalm 57:8 - Awake up, my glory; awake, psaltery and <u>harp</u>: I myself will awake early.

Psalm 71:22 - I will also praise thee with the psaltery, even thy truth, O my God: unto thee will I sing with the <u>harp</u>, O thou Holy One of Israel.

Psalm 81:2 - Take a psalm, and bring hither the timbrel, the pleasant <u>harp</u> with the psaltery.

Psalm 92:3 - Upon an instrument of ten strings, and upon the psaltery; upon the <u>harp</u> with a solemn sound.

Psalm 98:5 - Sing unto the Lord with the <u>harp</u>; with the <u>harp</u>, and the voice of a psalm.

Psalm 108:2 - Awake, psaltery and <u>harp</u>: I myself will awake early.

Psalm 137:2 - We hanged our <u>harps</u> upon the willows in the midst thereof.

Psalm 147:7 - Sing unto the Lord with thanksgiving; sing praise upon the <u>harp</u> unto our God:

Psalm 149:3 - Let them praise his name in the dance: let them sing praises unto him with the timbrel and <u>harp</u>.

Psalm 150:3 - Praise him with the sound of the trumpet: praise him with the psaltery and harp.

Isaiah 5:12 - And the harp, and the viol, the tabret, and pipe, and wine, are in their feasts: but they regard not the work of the Lord, neither consider the operation of his hands.

Isaiah 16:11 - Wherefore my bowels shall sound like an harp for Moab, and mine inward parts for Kirharesh.

Isaiah 23:16 - Take an harp, go about the city, thou harlot that hast been forgotten; make sweet melody, sing many songs, that thou mayest be remembered.

Isaiah 24:8 - The mirth of tabrets ceaseth, the noise of them that rejoice endeth, the joy of the harp ceaseth.

Isaiah 30:32 - And in every place where the grounded staff shall pass, which the Lord shall lay upon him, it shall be with tabrets and harps: and in battles of shaking will he fight with it.

Ezekiel 26:13 - And I will cause the noise of thy songs to cease; and the sound of thy harps shall be no more heard.

Daniel 3:5 - That at what time ye hear the sound of the cornet, flute, harp, sackbut, psaltery, dulcimer, and all kinds of musick, ye fall down and worship the golden image that Nebuchadnezzar the king hath set up:

Daniel 3:7 - Therefore at that time, when all the people heard the sound of the cornet, flute, harp, sackbut, psaltery,and all kinds of musick, all the people, the nations, and the languages, fell down and worshipped the golden image that Nebuchadnezzar the king had set up.

Daniel 3:10 - Thou, O king, hast made a decree, that every man that shall hear the sound of the cornet, flute, harp, sackbut, psaltery, and dulcimer, and all kinds of musick, shall fall down and worship the golden image:

Daniel 3:15 - Now if ye be ready that at what time ye hear the sound of the cornet, flute, harp, sackbut, psaltery, and dulcimer, and all kinds of musick, ye fall down and worship the image which I have made; well: but if ye worship not, ye shall be cast the same hour into the midst of a burning fiery furnace; and who is that God that shall deliver you out of my hands?

I Corinthians 14:7 - And even things without life giving sound, whether pipe or harp, except they give a distinction in the sounds, how shall it be known what is piped or harped?

Revelation 5:8 - And when he had taken the book, the four beasts and four and twenty elders fell down before the Lamb, having every one of them harps, and golden vials full of odours, which are the prayers of saints.

Revelation 14:2 - And I heard a voice from heaven, as the voice of many waters, and as the voice of a great thunder: and I heard the voice of harpers harping with their harps:

Revelation 15:2 - And I saw as it were a sea of glass mingled with fire: and them that had gotten the victory over the beast, and over his image, and over his mark, and over the number of his name, stand on the sea of glass, having the harps of God.

harped

I Corinthians 14:7 - And even things without life giving sound, whether pipe or harp, except they give a distinction in the sounds, how shall it be known what is piped or harped?

harpers

Revelation 14:2 - And I heard a voice from heaven, as the voice of many waters, and as the voice of a great thunder: and I heard the voice of harpers harping with their harps:

Revelation 18:22 - And the voice of harpers, and musicians, and of pipers and trumpeters, shall be heard no more at all in thee; and no craftsman, of whatsoever craft he be, shall be found any more in thee; and the sound of a millstone shall be heard no more at all in thee;

harping

Revelation 14:2 - And I heard a voice from heaven, as the voice of many waters,and as the voice of a great thunder: and I heard the voice of harpers harping with their harps:

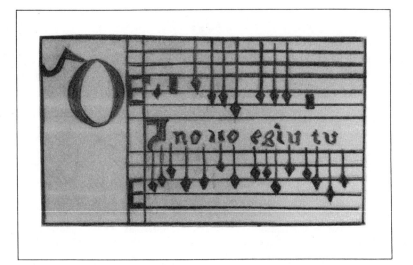

hymn(s)

A hymn is a song of praise to God, and is a musical foundation of many churches. In contemporary church services, hymns are sung with or without accompaniment. Historically, the hymn has usually been rather simple, often with repeated verses to the same melody and harmony. This characteristic would be necessary to involve an entire congregation, as hymn-singing often does--many of the members of which are not proficient at reading music. This is in contrast to the more complex musical arrangements often sung by a church's choir, which is made up of variously trained musicians who rehearse. Hymn tunes have been notated and handed down through the centuries, and sometimes have been used as a generative basis for the composition of extended musical works, both instrumental and vocal.

The scholarly specialty of hymnology has developed, whereby persons apply objective methods to the study of hymns and related musics. Such aspects include history, theoretical analysis, and study of the texts. Hymnologists are quite often interested in producing historically accurate editions in their research, and usually are more interested in "what actually was" in regard to hymn-type music of the past, rather than in "what should be," which the Bible suggests. As such, the area of hymnology is an extremely important adjunct to the contemporary church as an institution, by helping to delineate the past and thus aiding to define the present and future, using aspects of the scientific method in the study of substantive religious music. This is perhaps an area where the technological and the spiritual can work to mutual benefit in pursuing the "harmony of the cosmos" as philosophized by the writers of ancient Greece. Since the advent of the field of natural science a few centuries ago, and the resulting emphasis on technological "advancement" in Western society which is now drifting to Eastern society and the "third world," a significant conflict has been present between the religious, or spiritual, and the scientific, or technological. Hymnology, the method of applying an attempt at objective perspective to the stuff of religion--in this case, hymn music--can perhaps serve as an area

30

of confluence of previously combative points of view, and promote a better world here on Earth for the 21st Century.

Matthew 26:30 - And when they had sung an <u>hymn</u>, they went out into the mount of Olives.

Mark 14:26 - And when they had sung an <u>hymn</u>, they went out into the mount of Olives.

Ephesians 5:19 - Speaking to yourselves in psalms and <u>hymns</u> and spiritual songs, singing and making melody in your heart to the Lord;

Colossians 3:16 - Let the word of Christ dwell in you richly in all wisdom; teaching and admonishing one another in psalms and <u>hymns</u> and spiritual songs, singing with grace in your hearts to the Lord.

instrument(s)

Many of the various references to "instruments" in the Bible do indeed refer to musical instruments. With some references, it is unclear if musical instruments are discussed, or if a generic meaning is intended, as in "instruments of the tabernacle." Some references clearly do not infer musicality, and these notations have been omitted.

Perhaps the most basic musical instrument is the human voice, and one may note that the most numerous terms in this book refer to vocal music such as "sing," "song," et cetera. Many persons over the centuries have concluded that the most pure, or holy, of musical instruments is that of the voice, and some religious groups allow only vocal music within their service. Interestingly, in the Baroque era of European classical music--the beginning of our "modern" era--many musicians and lovers of music felt that, indeed, the most "pure" form of music was instrumental, that is, non-vocal. This philosophy extended from the idea that words in music tend to "clutter up" the purely musical sounds which are the emanation of the soul.

Proceeding from the prior statement that this editor/author considers the human voice as the most basic of musical instruments, this assumption is based on the idea that the voice, produced by the human body directly and coming from within, is the most intimate of musical instruments. Thus it would be considered the most emotional of instruments, for descriptive purposes. Following this line of thinking, the percussion instruments--the bells, cymbals, tabrets, and timbrels--would be considered the least intimate of musical instruments, since they involve striking percussively--a rather aggressive, in contrast to an intimately emotional, action. Other instruments would be between these two extremes on the scale of emotionality and intimate method of production. It is no accident that the human voice can thus produce sensuality in music, whether religious or non-religious in nature, and the percussion can produce the most rhythmic music of all instruments--often without important melodic and harmonic elements. A similar line of thinking might conclude that the voice is the most human, spiritual, and thus "musical" of instruments, and in hierarchical order the strings, winds, and percussion would follow, with the latter being the most aboriginal, physical,

32

and least artistic in nature. This order of hierarchy seems to have occurred in the fine art of classical music in Western civilization the past two thousand years, with perhaps the 20th Century producing a liberation of sorts from these values.

This hierarchy of values does not seem to exist traditionally in Chinese, Japanese, Indian and African cultures. Nor does it seem to be inferred from the Biblical Scriptures, as one may notice by reading the various musical references. Generally, Biblical references to instruments and music seem to equate the various aspects of human musicality as pretty much on the same level. At times the harp is said to produce "noise," for example, while music in general is associated variously with the entire range of emotions from ecstasy to extreme sadness. Indeed, mirth and lamenting can be expressed musically according to the Bible, and thus the instruments of men and women can be used to serve and to aid in worshipping God.

Exodus 25:9 - According to all that I shew thee, after the pattern of the tabernacle, and the pattern of all the instruments thereof, even so shall ye make it.

Numbers 3:8 - And they shall keep all the instruments of the tabernacle of the congregation, and the charge of the children of Israel, to do the service of the tabernacle.

Numbers 4:12 - And they shall take all the instruments of ministry, wherewith they minister in the sanctuary, and put them in a cloth of blue, and cover them with a covering of badgers' skins, and shall put them on a bar:

Numbers 7:1 - And it came to pass on the day that Moses had fully set up the tabernacle, and had anointed it, and sanctified it, and all the instruments thereof, both the altar and all the vessels thereof, and had anointed them, and sanctified them;

Numbers 31:6 - And Moses sent them to the war, a thousand of every tribe, them and Phinehas the son of Eleazar the priest, to the war, with the holy instruments, and the trumpets to blow in his hand.

I Samuel 18:6 - And it came to pass as they came, when David was returned from the slaughter of the Philistine, that the women came out of all cities of Israel, singing and dancing, to meet king Saul, with tabrets, with joy, and with instruments of musick.

II Samuel 6:5 - And David and all the house of Israel played before the Lord on all manner of instruments made of fir wood, even on harps, and on psalteries, and on timbrels, and on cornets, and on cymbals.

I Chronicles 9:29 - Some of them also were appointed to oversee the vessels, and all the instruments of the sanctuary, and the fine flour, and the wine, and the oil, and the frankincense, and the spices.

I Chronicles 16:16 - And David spake to the chief of the Levites to appoint their brethren to be the singers with instruments of musick, psalteries and harps and cymbals, sounding, by lifting up the voice with joy.

I Chronicles 16:42 - And with them Heman and Jeduthun with trumpets and cymbals for those that should make a sound, and with musical instruments of God. And the sons of Jeduthun were porters.

I Chronicles 23:5 - Moreover four thousand were porters; and four thousand praised the Lord with the instruments which I made, said David, to praise therewith.

I Chronicles 28:14 - He gave of gold by weight for things of gold, for all instruments of all manner of service; silver also for all instruments of silver by weight, for all instruments of every kind of service:

II Chronicles 4:16 - The pots also, and the shovels, and the fleshhooks, and all their instruments, did Huram his father make to king Solomon for the house of the Lord of bright brass.

II Chronicles 5:1 - Thus all the work that Solomon made for the house of the Lord was finished: and Solomon brought in all the things that David his father had dedicated; and the silver, and the gold, and all the instruments, put he among the treasures of the house of God.

II Chronicles 5:13 - It came even to pass, as the trumpeters and singers were as one, to make one sound to be heard in praising and thanking the Lord; and when they lifted up their voice with the trumpets and cymbals and instruments of musick, and praised the Lord, saying, For he is good; for his mercy endureth for ever: that then the house was filled with a cloud, even the house of the Lord;

II Chronicles 7:6 - And the priests waited on their offices; the Levites also with instruments of musick of the Lord, which David the king had made to praise the Lord, because his mercy endureth for ever, when David praised by their ministry; and the priests sounded trumpets before them, and all Israel stood.

II Chronicles 23:13 - And she looked, and, behold, the king stood at his pillar at the entering in, and the princes and the trumpets by the king: and all the people of the land rejoiced, and sounded with trumpets, also the singers with instruments of musick, and such as taught to sing praise. Then Athaliah rent her clothes, and said, Treason, Treason.

II Chronicles 29:26 - And the Levites stood with the <u>instruments</u> of David, and the priests with the trumpets.

II Chronicles 29:27 - And Hezekiah commanded to offer the burnt offering upon the altar. And when the burnt offering began, the song of the Lord began also with the trumpets, and with the <u>instruments</u> ordained by David king of Israel.

II Chronicles 30:21 - And the child of Israel that were present at Jerusalem kept the feast of unleavened bread seven days with great gladness: and the Levites and the priests praised the Lord day by day, singing with loud <u>instruments</u> unto the Lord.

II Chronicles 34:12 - And the men did the work faithfully: and the overseers of them were Jahath and Obadiah, the Levites, of the sons of Merari; and Zechariah and Meshullam, of the sons of the Kohathites, to set it forward; and other of the Levites, all that could skill of <u>instruments</u> of musick.

Nehemiah 12:36 - And his brethren, Shemaiah, and Azarael, Milalai, Gilalai, Maai, Nethaneel, and Judah, Hanani, with the musical <u>instruments</u> of David the man of God, and Ezra the scribe before them.

Psalm 68;25 - The singers went before, the players on <u>instruments</u> followed after; among them were the damsels playing with timbrels.

Psalm 87:7 - As well the singers as the payers on <u>instruments</u> shall be there: all my springs are in thee.

Psalm 150:4 - Praise him with the timbrel and dance: praise him with stringed <u>instruments</u> and organs.

Ecclesiastes 2:8 - I gathered me also silver and gold, and the peculiar treasure of kings and of the provinces: I gat me men singers and women singers, and the delights of the sons of men, as musical <u>instruments</u>, and that of all sorts.

Isaiah 38:20 - The Lord was ready to save me: therefore we will sing my songs to the stringed <u>instruments</u> all the days of our life in the house of the Lord.

Ezekiel 33:32 - And, lo, thou art unto them as a very lovely song of one that hath a pleasant voice, and can play well on an <u>instrument</u>: for they hear thy words, but they do them not.

Daniel 6:18 - Then the king went to his palace, and passed the night fasting: neither were <u>instruments</u> of musick brought before him: and his sleep went from him.

Amos 6:5 - That chant to the sound of the viol, and invent to themselves <u>instruments</u> of musick, like David;

Habakkuk 3:19 - The Lord God is my strength, and he will make my feet like hinds' feet, and he will make me to walk upon mine high places. To the chief singer on my stringed <u>instruments</u>.

Zechariah 11:15 - And the Lord said unto me, Take unto thee yet the <u>instruments</u> of a foolish shepherd.

instrument of ten strings

If only we could see a picture of the instrument of ten strings mentioned in various parts of the book of Psalms! We can only guess what it looked like. Some questions that might arise are:

1) Was it bowed or plucked?
2) Was it tuned to ten different pitches, or did it have five strings that were played, with an equal number of strings that vibrated sympathetically?
3) What did its soundbox look like?
4) What shape was the instrument?
5) What did it sound like?
6) What kind of relative pitch sequence was it tuned to?
7) How was the characteristic music of the instrument of ten strings comparable to and different from the music played by the harp and the viol of that time?
8) Furthermore, what were the essential differences, if any, between "sacred" and "secular" music of Biblical times? Was there indeed such a division, as there was in later centuries?

Unfortunately, this editor/author can offer very little in the way of answers to the preceding questions. About the only guess that I would venture is that perhaps the instrument was plucked, rather than bowed. It is interesting to wonder what indeed might be the possible answers to the other questions. An instrument of ten strings would produce rather complex music for analysis by music theorists, if the instrument's music were notated and/or recorded. Theorists would be able to study scalar material, tonal centers, form, and rhythm, as they do with later notated music. However, we can only wonder, as was mentioned, at what might have existed, and hopefully in the process gain a genuine appreciation of the accomplishments of pre-industrial men and women.

Psalm 33:2 - Praise the Lord with harp: sing unto him with the psaltery and an instrument of ten strings.

Psalm 92:3 - Upon an <u>instrument</u> <u>of</u> <u>ten</u> <u>strings</u>, and upon the psaltery; upon the harp with a solemn sound.

Psalm 144:9 - I will sing a new song unto thee, O God: upon a psaltery and an <u>instrument</u> <u>of</u> <u>ten</u> <u>strings</u> will I sing praises unto thee.

melody

Perhaps the most generally loved and remembered aspect of music through the ages is melody. For the modern music theorist, melody is only one of several facets of musical composition that are studied in depth, along with rhythm, form, harmony, and pertinent aspects of sound. For the generally untrained observer, however, melody remains supreme as the singular facet of music that is easiest to remember, to relate to, and to appreciate. It is fitting, then, that in these four excerpts from the Bible, melody is inferred as the synonym of musical beauty.

Isaiah 23:16 - Take an harp, go about the city, thou harlot that hast been forgotten; make sweet melody, sing many songs, that thou mayest be remembered.

Isaiah 51:3 - For the Lord shall comfort Zion: he will comfort all her waste places; and he will make her wilderness like Eden, and her desert like the garden of the Lord; joy and gladness shall be found therein, thanksgiving, and the voice of melody.

Amos 5:23 - Take thou away from me the noise of thy songs; for I will not hear the melody of thy voice.

Ephesians 5:19 - Speaking to yourselves in psalms and hymns and spiritual songs, singing and making melody in your heart to the Lord;

musical

It is evident from these three excerpts using the adjective "musical," that such instruments were considered quite worthy for assistance in the worship of God, according to the Bible. Of course David is associated with things musical more than any other royalty mentioned in the Scriptures, and it is perhaps a significant Biblical message that David is best remembered for his exploits in the field of music in the service of God, rather than for his accomplishments on the battlefield.

I Chronicles 16:42 - And with them Heman and Jeduthun with trumpets and cymbals for those that should make a sound, and with musical instruments of God.

Nehemiah 12:36 - And his brethren, Shemaiah, and Azarael, Milalai, Gilalai, Maai, Nethaneel, and Judah, Hanani, with the musical instruments of David the man of God, and Ezra the scribe before them.

Ecclesiastes 2:8 - I gathered me also silver and gold, and the peculiar treasure of kings and of the provinces: I gat me men singers and women singers, and the delights of the sons of men, as musical instruments, and that of all sorts.

Musician

No less than 55 of the 150 Psalms are headed with reference to a chief musician. The most common heading is "To the chief Musician, A Psalm of David," although there are several variations. It is known that "psalm" is often synonymous with "song," and thus it would be reasonable to associate a psalm with a producer of song, that is, a musician. It is interesting, for the scholarly inquisitive person, to notice the various headings and references in their sometimes contrasting format.

Psalm 4 - To the chief Musician on Neginoth, A Psalm of David.

Psalm 5 - To the chief Musician upon Nehiloth, A Psalm of David.

Psalm 6 -To the chief Musician on Neginoth upon Sheminith, A Psalm of David.

Psalm 8 - To the chief Musician upon Gittith, A Psalm of David.

Psalm 9 - To the chief Musician upon Muthlabben, A Psalm of David.

Psalm 11 - To the chief Musician, A Psalm of David.

Psalm 12 - To the chief Musician upon Sheminith, A Psalm of David.

Psalm 13 - To the chief Musician, A Psalm of David.

Psalm 14 - To the chief Musician, A Psalm of David.

Psalm 18 - To the chief Musician, A Psalm of David, the servant of the Lord, who spake unto the Lord the words of this song in the day that the Lord delivered him from the hand of all his enemies, and from the hand of Saul: And he said,

Psalm 19 - To the chief Musician, A Psalm of David.

Psalm 20 - To the chief Musician, A Psalm of David.

Psalm 21 - To the chief Musician, A Psalm of David.

Psalm 22 - To the chief Musician upon Aijeleth Shahar, A Psalm of David.

Psalm 31 - To the chief Musician, A Psalm of David.

Psalm 36 - To the chief Musician, A Psalm of David the servant of the Lord.

Psalm 39 - To the chief Musician, even to Jeduthun, A Psalm of David.

Psalm 40 - To the chief Musician, A Psalm of David.

Psalm 41 - To the chief Musician, A Psalm of David.

Psalm 42 - To the chief Musician, Maschil, for the sons of Korah.

Psalm 44 - To the chief Musician for the sons of Korah, Maschil.

Psalm 45 - To the chief Musician upon Shoshannim, for the sons of Korah, Maschil, A Song of loves.

Psalm 46 - To the chief Musician for the sons of Korah, A Song upon Alamoth.

Psalm 47 - To the chief Musician, A Psalm for the sons of Korah.

Psalm 49 - To the chief Musician, A Psalm for the sons of Korah.

Psalm 51 - To the chief Musician, A Psalm of David, when Nathan the prophet came unto him, after he had gone in to Bath-sheba.

Psalm 52 - To the chief Musician, Maschil, A Psalm of David, when Doeg the Edomite came and told Saul, and said unto him, David is come to the house of Ahimelech.

Psalm 53 - To the chief Musician upon Mahalath, Maschil, A Psalm of David.

Psalm 54 - To the chief Musician on Neginoth, Maschil, A Psalm of David, when the Ziphims came and said to Saul, Doth not David hide himself with us?

Psalm 55 - To the chief Musician on Neginoth, Maschil, A Psalm of David.

Psalm 56 - To the chief Musician upon Jonath-elem-rechokim, Michtam of David, when the Philistines took him in Gath.

Psalm 57 - To the chief Musician, Al-taschith, Michtam of David, when he fled from Saul in the cave.

Psalm 58 - To the chief Musician, Al-taschith, Michtam of David.

Psalm 59 - To the chief Musician, Al-taschith, Michtam of David; when Saul sent, and they watched the house to kill him.

Psalm 60 - To the chief <u>Musician</u> upon Shushan-eduth, Michtam of David, to teach; when he strove with Aram-naharaim and with Aram-zobah, when Joab returned, and smote of Edom in the valley of salt twelve thousand.

Psalm 61 - To the chief <u>Musician</u> upon Neginah, A Psalm of David.

Psalm 62 - To the chief <u>Musician,</u> to Jeduthun, A Psalm of David.

Psalm 64 - To the chief <u>Musician,</u> A Psalm of David.

Psalm 65 - To the chief <u>Musician,</u> A Psalm and Song of David.

Psalm 66 - To the chief <u>Musician,</u> A Song or Psalm.

Psalm 67 - To the chief <u>Musician</u> on Neginoth, A Psalm or Song.

Psalm 68 - To the chief <u>Musician,</u> A Psalm or Song of David.

Psalm 69 - To the chief <u>Musician</u> upon Shoshannim, A Psalm of David.

Psalm 70 - To the chief <u>Musician,</u> A Psalm of David, to bring to remembrance.

Psalm 75 - To the chief <u>Musician,</u> Al-taschith, A Psalm or Song of Asaph.

Psalm 76 - To the chief <u>Musician</u> on Neginoth, Psalm or Song of Asaph.

Psalm 77 - To the chief <u>Musician,</u> to Jeduthun, A Psalm of Asaph.

Psalm 80 - To the chief <u>Musician</u> upon Shoshannim-Eduth, A Psalm of Asaph.

Psalm 81 - To the chief <u>Musician</u> upon Gittith, A Psalm of Asaph.

Psalm 84 - To the chief <u>Musician</u> upon Gittith, A Psalm for the sons of Korah.

Psalm 85 - To the chief <u>Musician,</u> A Psalm for the sons of Korah.

Psalm 88 - A Song of Psalm for the sons of Korah, to the chief <u>Musician</u> upon Mahalath Leannoth, Maschil of Heman the Ezrahite.

Psalm 109 - To the chief <u>Musician,</u> A Psalm of David.

Psalm 139 - To the chief <u>Musician,</u> A Psalm of David.

Psalm 140 - To the chief <u>Musician,</u> A Psalm of David.

<u>musicians</u>

Interestingly, the plural generic term "musicians" appears only once in the Holy Bible, and then in the last book of the New Testament! Even the specific term "harpers" appears twice. Decidedly, most references are to specific instruments or types of music, or to terms that describe the act of performing music. However, as one might notice elsewhere in this listing, the term "singer(s)" is plentiful throughout the Bible. Perhaps it can be assumed that "singer" would possibly be equated with "musician" in a generic sense-- again, based on the idea that instrumental music is but an extension of the voice, if in another idiom. It might also be assumed that many musicians "doubled" on various instruments in addition to singing. Pursuing this latter idea, it is reasonable to speculate that the area of specialization had not yet occurred in Biblical times, and thus "musicians" might sing, perform on an instrument or instruments, and perhaps also dance.

Revelation 18:22 - And the voice of harpers, and <u>musicians,</u> and of pipers, and trumpeters, shall be heard no more at all in thee; and no craftsman, of whatsoever craft he be, shall be found any more in thee; and the sound of a millstone shall be heard no more at all in thee;

musick

The 17th-Century English spelling of "musick" is only slightly different from the modern spelling. The art and science of music has been around as long as we have recorded history, and probably longer. The information explosion that has occurred during the 20th Century has brought to light a kind of awareness that has not always been present in all societies and cultures. For example, the present day musician or music lover might appreciate classical European music of recent centuries, yet be relatively aware of jazz, sacred music, and "exotic" music of Asia.

Music has had various definitions at various times and places. It can be defined as the expression of the human soul, as instigated by the devil, and broadly as "organized sound in time," which would include the rustling of leaves on a windy day (presumably with Nature or God being the "organizer" in this latter instance). The ancient Greeks spoke of the "harmony of the universe," inferring generally that certain principles of organization were shared in music with those of the universe as a whole. Furthermore, the ancient Greeks were concerned with the ethos, or the moral qualities and effects of music. This concern is shared in the present day by those who feel that certain kinds of music predispose a person to aggression and peace variously. In Western art music history, there has seemed to be an alternation of two opposing emphases in music, labeled here as the emotional and the intellectual, or the romantic and the classic. In the various "classic" periods, musical emphases have been on structure, organization, finesse, and perhaps restraint. In the various "romantic" periods the musical emphases have been on expression, fervor, individuality or personality, and extreme contrast.

We can only speculate what music was like in Biblical times. Judging from the references to music in the Scriptures, however, one can make the educated guess that there were probably many kinds of musics among various individuals, groups, and cultures. Presumably there were variations within groups, which the politically analytical observer might describe as "liberal" and "conservative" in nature. Thus one person's music of adoration might sound boring or silly to someone else. The editor/author's approach herewith continues to include commentary in a subsidiary manner, while allowing the King James Version of the holy Scriptures to speak for itself.

I Samuel 18:6 - And it came to pass as they came, when David was returned from the slaughter of the Philistine, that the women came out of all cities of Israel, singing and dancing, to meet king Saul, with tabrets, with joy, and with instruments of <u>musick</u>.

I Chronicles 16:16 - And David spake to the chief of the Levites to appoint their brethren to be the singers with instruments of <u>musick</u>, psalteries and harps and cymbals, sounding, by lifting up the voice with joy.

II Chronicles 5:13 - It came even to pass, as the trumpeters and singers were as one, to make one sound to be heard in praising and thanking the Lord; and when they lifted up their voice with the trumpets and cymbals and instruments of <u>musick</u>, and praised the Lord, saying, For he is good; for his mercy endureth for ever: that then the house was filled with a cloud, even the house of the Lord;

II Chronicles 7:6 - And the priests waited on their offices: the Levites also with instruments of <u>musick</u> of the Lord, which David the king had made to praise the Lord, because his mercy endureth for ever, when David praised by their ministry; and the priests sounded trumpets before them, and all Israel stood.

II Chronicles 23:13 - And she looked, and, behold, the king stood at his pillar at the entering in, and the princes and the trumpets by the king: and all the people of the land rejoiced, and sounded with trumpets, also the singers with instruments of <u>musick</u>, and such as taught to sing praise. Then Athaliah rent her clothes, and said, Treason, Treason.

II Chronicles 34:12 - And the men did the work faithfully: and the overseers of them were Jahath and Obadiah, the Levites, of the sons of Merari; and Zechariah and Meshullam, of the sons of the Kohathites, to set it forward; and other of the Levites, all that could skill of instruments of <u>musick</u>.

Ecclesiastes 12:4 - And the doors shall be shut in the streets, when the sound of the grinding is low, and he shall rise up at the voice of the bird, and all the daughters of <u>musick</u> shall be brought low;

Lamentations 3:63 - Behold their sitting down, and their rising up; I am their <u>musick</u>.

Lamentations 5:14 - The elders have ceased from the gate, the young men from their <u>musick</u>.

Daniel 3:5 - That at what time ye hear the sound of the cornet, flute, harp, sackbut, psaltery, dulcimer, and all kinds of <u>musick</u>, ye fall down and worship the golden image that Nebuchadnezzar the king hath set up:

Daniel 3:7 - Therefore at that time, when all the people heard the sound of the cornet, flute, harp, sackbut, psaltery, and all kinds of <u>musick</u>, all the people, the nations, and the languages, fell down and worshipped the golden image that Nebuchadnezzar the king had set up.

Daniel 3:10 - Thou, O king, hast made a decree, that every man that shall hear the sound of the cornet, flute, harp, sackbut, psaltery, and dulcimer, and all kinds of <u>musick</u>, shall fall down and worship the golden image:

Daniel 3:15 - Now if ye be ready that at what time ye hear the sound of the cornet, flute, harp, sackbut, psaltery, and dulcimer, and all kinds of <u>musick</u>, ye fall down and worship the image which I have made; well: but if ye worship not, ye shall be cast the same hour into the midst of a burning fiery furnace; and who is that God that shall deliver you out of my hands?

Daniel 6:18 - Then the king went to his palace, and passed the night fasting: neither were instruments of <u>musick</u> brought before him: and his sleep went from him.

Amos 6:5 - That chant to the sound of the viol, and invent to themselves instruments of <u>musick</u>, like David;

Luke 15:25 - Now his elder son was in the field: and as he came and drew nigh to the house, he heard <u>musick</u> and dancing.

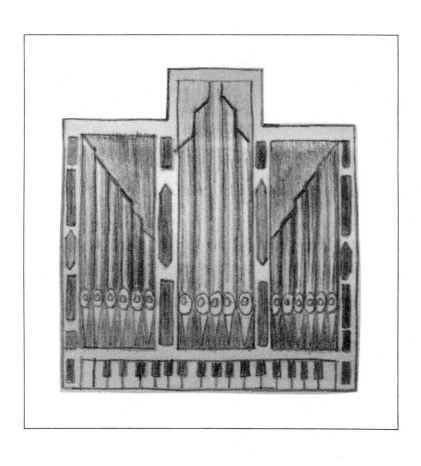

organ(s)

The predecessor of the organ as we know it has been around at least since the 2nd Century B.C., and itself was preceded by pan-pipes and similar instruments, some of which might have had external "bellows" of sorts perhaps operated by an assistant to the performer. Technical maturity of the instrument awaited the rise of industrialization and technological accomplishments of the past few centuries. In the 20th Century the organ is the most important musical instrument of many churches, and ranks next only to the human voice hierarchically as musical purveyor of ideas spiritual. Historians would debate whether the organ as a keyboard instrument existed in Biblical times, though the three references here listed from the Bible seem to indicate the strong possibility of its presence in a specific design perhaps of the organ type. Certainly, however, the organ was not of the importance for religious worship in Biblical times that it has risen to in the 20th and recent centuries in the Western world and elsewhere. The marvelous organ and keyboard music of Johann Sebastian Bach (1685-1750) and others has strongly influenced the high position the instrument holds in today's church. Indeed, the status enjoyed by this important musical instrument today was perhaps foreshadowed by the complimentary comments about the organ in the holy Scriptures.

Genesis 4:21 - And his brother's name was Jubal: he was the father of all such as handle the harp and <u>organ</u>.

Job 30:31 - My harp also turned to mourning, and my <u>organ</u> into the voice of them that weep.

Psalm 150:4 - Praise him with the timbrel and dance: praise him with stringed instruments and <u>organs</u>.

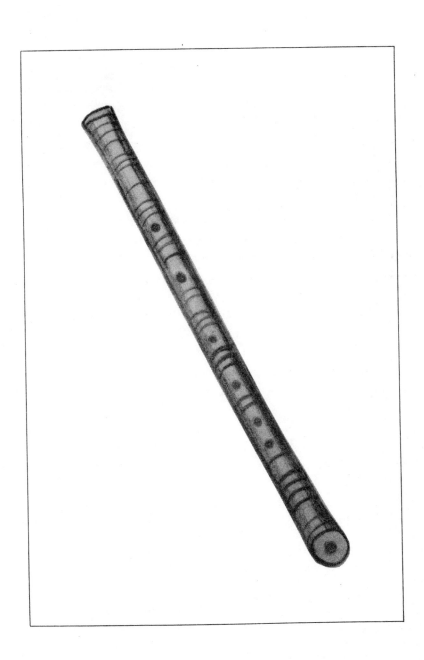

pipe(s)

The "pipe" can refer to a simple musical instrument made up of a hollow tube, with or without finger holes. Generically the designation can identify any of the various types of flute. As in similar instances throughout the Bible, we can only guess as to the differences between the indicated pipe and the flute. This editor/author suspects that early Biblical scholars did perceive a difference, and that most likely the Biblical pipe was of simpler construction than that of the flute of that era.

The mediaeval "pipe and tabor" are foreshadowed herein by the coupling of pipe and tabret. Beginning in the Middle Ages in Europe, perhaps as early as the 13th Century, a musician might hold the pipe in his or her left hand (it had finger holes), then strike the small tom-tom, or tabor, with a stick held in the right hand; in such instances the tabor was suspended by a string or rope around the performer's neck and shoulder. The Biblical tabret was a similar small tom-tom or drum, sometimes mentioned with the pipe. As with a few other terms, the pipe listed herein is usually, but not always, in reference to a musical instrument. "Pipers" and "piped" are of course extensions of the basic word "pipe."

I Samuel 10:5 - After that thou shalt come to the hill of God, where is the garrison of the Philistines: and it shall come to pass, when thou art come thither to the city, that thou shalt meet a company of prophets coming down from the high place with a psaltery, and a tabret, and a pipe, and a harp, before them; and they shall prophesy:

I Kings 1:40 - And all the people came up after him, and the people piped with pipes, and rejoiced with great joy, so that the earth rent with the sound of them.

Isaiah 5:12 - And the harp, and the viol, the tabret, and pipe, and wine, are in their feasts: but they regard not the work of the Lord, neither consider the operation of his hands.

Isaiah 30:29 - Ye shall have a song, as in the night when a holy solemnity is kept; and gladness of heart, as when one goeth with a pipe to come into the mountain of the Lord, to the mighty One of Israel.

Jeremiah 48:36 - Therefore mine heart shall sound for Moab like pipes, and mine heart shall sound like pipes for the men of Kir-heres: because the riches that he hath gotten are perished.

Ezekiel 28:13 - Thou hast been in Eden the garden of God; every previous stone was thy covering, the sardius, topaz, and the diamond, the beryl, and onyx, and the jasper, the sapphire, the emerald, and the carbuncle, and gold: the workmanship of thy tabrets and of thy <u>pipes</u> was prepared in thee in the day that thou wast created.

Zechariah 4:2 - And said unto me,What seest thou? And I said, I have looked, and behold a candlestick all of gold, with a bowl upon the top of it, and his seven lamps thereon, and seven <u>pipes</u> to the seven lamps, which are upon the top thereof:

Zechariah 4:12 - And I answered again, and said unto him, What be these two olive branches which through the two golden <u>pipes</u> empty the golden oil out of themselves?

I Corinthians 14:7 - And even things without life giving sound, whether <u>pipe</u> or harp, except they give a distinction in the sounds, how shall it be known what is piped or harped?

piped

I Kings 1:40 - And all the people came up after him,and the people <u>piped</u> with pipes, and rejoiced with great joy, so that the earth rent with the sound of them.

Matthew 11:17 - And saying, We have <u>piped</u> unto you, and ye have not danced; we have mourned unto you, and ye have not lamented.

Luke 7:32 - They are like unto children sitting in the marketplace, and calling one to another, and saying, We have <u>piped</u> unto you, and ye have not danced; we have mourned to you, and ye have not wept.

I Corinthians 14:7 - And even things without life giving sound, whether pipe or harp, except they give a distinction in the sounds, how shall it be known what is <u>piped</u> or harped?

pipers

Revelation 18:22 - And the voice of harpers, and musicians, and of <u>pipers</u>, and trumpeters, shall be heard no more at all in thee; and no craftsmen, of whatsoever craft he be, shall be found any more in thee; and the sound of a millstone shall be heard no more at all in thee;

52

Psalm

The general definition of a psalm is that it is a sacred song or hymn, many of which originated in the book of Psalms in the Holy Bible. All of these songs have probably been set to music at various times in the past few hundred years, the best known examples being the psalters of centuries past. The present listing has five headings: Psalm, psalm, psalmist, Psalms, and psalms.

Psalm 3 - A Psalm of David, when he fled from Absalom his son.

Psalm 4 - To the chief Musician upon Neginoth, A Psalm of David.

Psalm 5 - To the chief Musician upon Neginoth, A Psalm of David.

Psalm 6 - To the chief Musician on Neginoth upon Sheminith, A Psalm of David.

Psalm 8 - To the chief Musician upon Gittith, A Psalm of David.

Psalm 9 - To the chief Musician upon Muthlabben, A Psalm of David.

Psalm 11 - To the chief Musician, A Psalm of David.

Psalm 12 - To the chief Musician upon Sheminith, A Psalm of David.

Psalm 13 - To the chief Musician, A Psalm of David.

Psalm 14 - To the chief Musician, A Psalm of David.

Psalm 15 - A Psalm of David.

Psalm 18 - To the chief Musician, A Psalm of David, the servant of the Lord, who spake unto the Lord the words of this song in the day that the Lord delivered him from the hand of all his enemies, and from the hand of Saul: And he said,

Psalm 19 - To the chief Musician, A Psalm of David.

Psalm 20 - To the chief Musician, A Psalm of David.

Psalm 21 - To the chief Musician, A Psalm of David.

Psalm 22 - To the chief Musician upon Aijeleth Shahar, A Psalm of David.

Psalm 23 - A Psalm of David.

Psalm 24 - A <u>Psalm</u> of David.

Psalm 25 - A <u>Psalm</u> of David.

Psalm 26 - A <u>Psalm</u> of David.

Psalm 27 - A <u>Psalm</u> of David.

Psalm 28 - A <u>Psalm</u> of David.

Psalm 29 - A <u>Psalm</u> of David.

Psalm 30 - A <u>Psalm</u> and Song at the dedication of the house of David.

Psalm 31 - To the chief Musician, A <u>Psalm</u> of David.

Psalm 32 - A <u>Psalm</u> of David, Maschil.

Psalm 34 - A <u>Psalm</u> of David, when he changed his behaviour before Abimelech; who drove him away, and he departed.

Psalm 35 - A <u>Psalm</u> of David.

Psalm 36 - To the chief Musician, A <u>Psalm</u> of David the servant of the Lord.

Psalm 37 - A <u>Psalm</u> of David.

Psalm 38 - A <u>Psalm</u> of David, to bring to remembrance.

Psalm 39 - To the chief Musician, even to Jeduthun, A <u>Psalm</u> of David.

Psalm 40 - To the chief Musician, A <u>Psalm</u> of David.

Psalm 41 - To the chief Musician, A <u>Psalm</u> of David.

Psalm 47 - To the chief Musician, A <u>Psalm</u> for the sons of Korah.

Psalm 48 - A Song and <u>Psalm</u> for the sons of Korah.

Psalm 49 - To the chief Musician, A <u>Psalm</u> for the sons of Korah.

Psalm 50 - A <u>Psalm</u> of Asaph.

Psalm 51 - To the chief Musician, A <u>Psalm</u> of David, when Nathan the prophet came unto him, after he had gone in to Bath-sheba.

Psalm 52 - To the chief Musician, Maschil, A <u>Psalm</u> of David, when Doeg the Edomite came and told Saul, and said unto him, David is come to the house of Ahimelech.

Psalm 53 - To the chief Musician upon Mahalath, Maschil, A Psalm of David.

Psalm 54 - To the chief Musician on Neginoth, Maschil, A Psalm of David, when the Ziphims came and said to Saul, Doth not David hide himself with us?

Psalm 55 - To the chief Musician on Neginoth, Maschil, A Psalm of David.

Psalm 61 - To the chief Musician upon Neginah, A Psalm of David.

Psalm 62 - To the chief Musician, to Jeduthun, A Psalm of David.

Psalm 63 - A Psalm of David, when he was in the wilderness of Judah.

Psalm 64 - To the chief Musician, A Psalm of David.

Psalm 65 - To the chief Musician, A Psalm and Song of David.

Psalm 66 - To the chief Musician, A Song or Psalm.

Psalm 67 - To the chief Musician on Neginoth, A Psalm or Song.

Psalm 68 - To the chief Musician, a Psalm or Song of David.

Psalm 69 - To the chief Musician upon Shoshannim, A Psalm of David.

Psalm 70 - To the chief Musician, A Psalm of David, to bring to remembrance.

Psalm 72 - A Psalm for Solomon.

Psalm 73 - A Psalm of Asaph.

Psalm 75 - To the chief Musician, Al-taschith, A Psalm or Song of Asaph.

Psalm 76- To the chief Musician on Neginoth, A Psalm or Song of Asaph.

Psalm 77 - To the chief Musician, to Jeduthun, A Psalm of Asaph.

Psalm 79 - A Psalm of Asaph.

Psalm 80 - To the chief Musician upon Shoshannim-Eduth, A Psalm of Asaph.

Psalm 81 - To the chief Musician upon Gittith, A Psalm of Asaph.

Psalm 82 - A Psalm of Asaph.

Psalm 83 - A Song or <u>Psalm</u> of Asaph.

Psalm 84 - To the chief Musician upon Gittith, A <u>Psalm</u> for the sons of Korah.

Psalm 85 - To the chief Musician, A <u>Psalm</u> for the sons of Korah.

Psalm 87 - A <u>Psalm</u> or Song for the sons of Korah.

Psalm 88 - A Song or <u>Psalm</u> for the sons of Korah, to the chief Musician upon Mahalath Leannoth, Maschil of Heman the Ezrahite.

Psalm 92 - A <u>Psalm</u> or Song for the sabbath day.

Psalm 98 - A <u>Psalm</u>.

Psalm 100 - A <u>Psalm</u> of praise.

Psalm 101 - A <u>Psalm</u> of David.

Psalm 103 - A <u>Psalm</u> of David.

Psalm 108 - A Song or <u>Psalm</u> of David.

Psalm 109 - To the chief Musician, A <u>Psalm</u> of David.

Psalm 110 - A <u>Psalm</u> of David.

Psalm 138 - A <u>Psalm</u> of David.

Psalm 139 - To the chief Musician, A <u>Psalm</u> of David.

Psalm 140 - To the chief Musician, A <u>Psalm</u> of David.

Psalm 141 - A <u>Psalm</u> of David.

Psalm 143 - A <u>Psalm</u> of David.

Psalm 144 - A <u>Psalm</u> of David.

Psalm 145 - David's <u>Psalm</u> of praise.

psalm

I Chronicles 16:7 - Then on that day David delivered first this <u>psalm</u> to thank the Lord into the hand of Asaph and his brethren.

Psalm 81:2 - Take a <u>psalm</u>, and bring hither the timbrel, the pleasant harp with the psaltery.

Psalm 98:5 - Sing unto the Lord with the harp; with the harp, and the voice of a <u>psalm</u>.

Acts 13:33 - God hath fulfilled the same unto us their children, in that he hath raised up Jesus again; as it is also written in the second <u>psalm</u>, Thou art my Son, this day have I begotten thee.

Acts 13:35 - Wherefore he saith also in another <u>psalm</u>, Thou shalt not suffer thine Holy One to see corruption.

I Corinthians 14:26 - How is it then, brethren? When ye come together, every one of you hath a <u>psalm</u>, hath a doctrine, hath a tongue, hath a revelation, hath an interpretation. Let all things be done unto edifying.

psalmist

II Samuel 23:1 - Now these be the last words of David. David the son of Jesse said, and the man who was raised up on high, the anointed of the God of Jacob, and the sweet <u>psalmist</u> of Israel, said,

Psalms

Luke 20:42 - And David himself saith in the book of <u>Psalms</u>, The Lord said unto my Lord, Sit thou on my right hand.

Acts 1:20 - For it is written in the book of <u>Psalms</u>, Let his habitation be desolate, and let no man dwell therein: and his bishoprick let another take.

psalms

I Chronicles 16:9 - Sing unto him, sing <u>psalms</u> unto him, talk ye of all his wondrous works.

Psalm 95:2 - Let us come before his presence with thanksgiving, and make a joyful noise unto him with <u>psalms</u>.

Psalm 105:2 - Sing unto him, sing <u>psalms</u> unto him: talk ye of all his wondrous works.

Luke 24:44 - And he said unto them, These are the words which I spake unto you, while I was yet with you, that all things must be fulfilled, which were written in the law of Moses, and in the prophets, and in the <u>psalms</u>, concerning me.

Ephesians 5:19 - Speaking to yourselves in <u>psalms</u> and hymns and spiritual songs, singing and making melody in your heart to the Lord;

Colossians 3:16 - Let the word of Christ swell in you richly in all wisdom; teaching and admonishing one another in <u>psalms</u> and hymns and spiritual songs, singing with grace in your hearts to the Lord.

James 5:13 - Is any among you afflicted? let him pray. Is any merry? let him sing <u>psalms</u>.

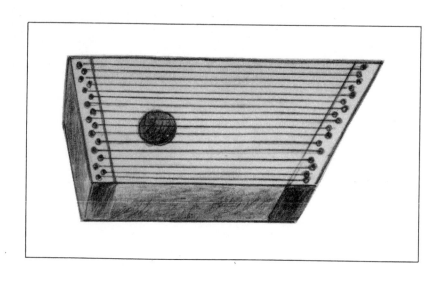

psaltery(ies)

The frequently mentioned psaltery was a stringed instrument that contained several strings stretched over a soundboard and perhaps tuned to definite pitches. The psaltery is usually discerned from the dulcimer by performance technique: the psaltery is plucked by the fingers, while the dulcimer is often struck with mallets or "hammers." Both instruments eventually developed into the harpsichord and pianoforte of modern Europe. A ten-stringed "psalterium" has been described in a letter attributed to St. Jerome (c. 330-420), and might be similarly the source of the Biblical "instrument of ten strings" included in this listing. The Biblical psaltery has been the inspiration for several beautiful artistic depictions, especially in painting, through the centuries.

I Samuel 10:5 - After that thou shalt come to the hill of God, where is the garrison of the Philistines: and it shall come to pass, when thou art come thither to the city, that thou shalt meet a company of prophets coming down from the high place with a psaltery, and a tabret, and a pipe, and a harp, before them; and they shall prophesy:

II Samuel 6:5 - And David and all the house of Israel played before the Lord on all manner of instruments made of fir wood, even on harps, and on psalteries, and on timbrels, and on cornets, and on cymbals.

I Kings 10:12 - And the king made of the almug trees pillars for the house of the Lord, and for the king's house, harps also and psalteries for singers: there came no such almug trees, nor were seen unto this day.

I Chronicles 18:8 - And David and all Israel played before God with all their might, and with singing, and with harps, and with psalteries, and with timbrels, and with cymbals, and with trumpets.

I Chronicles 15:16 - And David spake to the chief of the Levites to appoint their brethren to be the singers with instruments of musick, psalteries and harps and cymbals, sounding, by lifting up the voice with joy.

I Chronicles 15:20 - And Zechariah, and Aziel, and Shemiramoth, and Jehiel, and Unni, and Eliab, and Maaseiah, and Benaiah, with psalteries on Alamoth;

I Chronicles 15:28 - Thus all Israel brought up the ark of the covenant of the Lord with shouting, and with sound of the cornet, and with trumpets, and with cymbals, making a noise with psalteries and harps.

I Chronicles 16:5 - Asaph the chief, and next to him Zechariah, Jeiel, and Shemiramoth, and Jehiel, and Mattithiah, and Eliab, and Benaiah, and Obed-edom: and Jeiel with psalteries and with harps; but Asaph made a sound with cymbals.

I Chronicles 25:1 - Moreover David and the captains of the host separated to the service of the sons of Asaph, and of Heman, and of Jeduthun, who should prophesy with harps, with psalteries, and with cymbals: and the number of the workmen according to their service was:

I Chronicles 25:6 - All these were under the hands of their father for song in the house of the Lord, with cymbals, psalteries, and harps, for the service of the house of God, according to the king's order to Asaph, Jeduthun, and Heman.

II Chronicles 5:12 - Also the Levites which were the singers, all of them of Asaph, of Heman, of Jeduthun, with their sons and their brethren, being arrayed in white linen, having cymbals and psalteries and harps, stood at the east end of the altar, and with them an hundred and twenty priests sounding with trumpets:

II Chronicles 9:11 - And the king made of the algum trees terraces to the house of the Lord, and to the king's palace, and harps and psalteries for singers: and there were none such seen before in the land of Judah.

II Chronicles 20:28 - And they came to Jerusalem with psalteries and harps and trumpets unto the house of the Lord.

II Chronicles 29:25 - And he set the Levites in the house of the Lord with cymbals, with psalteries, and with harps, according to the commandment of David, and of Gad the king's seer, and Nathan the prophet: for so was the commandment of the Lord by his prophets.

Nehemiah 12:27 - And at the dedication of the wall of Jerusalem they sought the Levites out of all their places, to bring them to Jerusalem, to keep the dedication with gladness, both with thanksgivings, and with singing, with cymbals, psalteries, and with harps.

Psalm 33:2 - Praise the Lord with harp: sing unto him with the psaltery and an instrument of ten strings.

Psalm 57:8 - Awake up, my glory; awake, psaltery and harp: I myself will awake early.

Psalm 71:22 - I will also praise thee with the psaltery, even thy truth, O my God: unto thee will I sing with the harp, O thou Holy One of Israel.

Psalm 81:2 - Take a psalm, and bring hither the timbrel, the pleasant harp with the psaltery.

Psalm 92:3 - Upon an instrument of ten strings, and upon the <u>psaltery</u>; upon the harp with a solemn sound.

Psalm 108:2 - Awake, <u>psaltery</u> and harp: I myself will awake early.

Psalm 144:9 - I will sing a new song unto thee, O God: upon a <u>psaltery</u> and an instrument of ten strings will I sing praises unto thee.

Psalm 150:3 - Praise him with the sound of the trumpet: praise him with the <u>psaltery</u> and harp.

Daniel 3:5 - That at what time ye hear the sound of the cornet, flute, harp, sackbut, <u>psaltery</u>, dulcimer, and all kinds of musick, ye fall down and worship the golden image that Nebuchadnezzar the king hath set up:

Daniel 3:7 - Therefore at that time, when all the people heard the sound of the cornet, flute, harp, sackbut, <u>psaltery</u>, and all kinds of musick, all the people, the nations, and the languages, fell down and worshipped the golden image that Nebuchadnezzar the king had set up.

Daniel 3:10 - Thou, O king, has made a decree, that every man that shall hear the sound of the cornet, flute, harp, sackbut, <u>psaltery</u>, and dulcimer, and all kinds of musick, shall fall down and worship the golden image:

Daniel 3:15 - Now if ye be ready that at what time ye hear the sound of the cornet, flute, harp, sackbut, <u>psaltery</u>, and dulcimer, and all kinds of musick, ye fall down and worship the image which I have made; well: but if ye worship not, ye shall be cast the same hour into the midst of a burning fiery furnace; and who is that God that shall deliver you out of my hands?

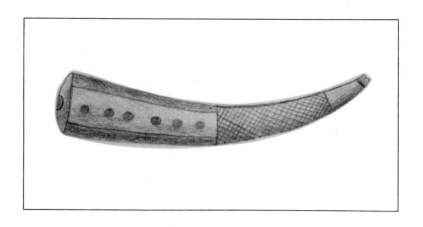

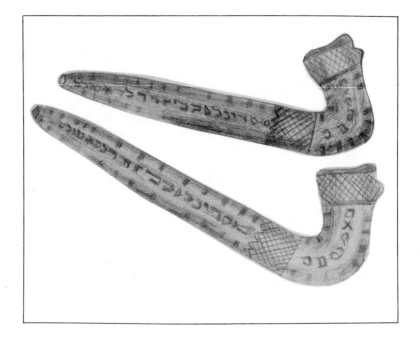

ram's horn

The ram's horn is today known as the shofar, or Jewish ceremonial horn. This ancient instrument, made from the animal's head adornment as indicated by its name, has perhaps been around for thirty centuries. It presently is used to announce the celebration of the Jewish New Year, producing usually only two harmonic sounds, nevertheless awe-inspiring in nature.

Joshua 6:5 - And it shall come to pass, that when they make a long blast with the ram's horn, and when ye hear the sound of the trumpet, all the people shall shout with a great shout; and the wall of the city shall fall down flat, and the people shall ascend up every man straight before him.

rams' horns

Joshua 6:4 - And seven priests shall bear before the ark seven trumpets of rams' horns: and the seventh day ye shall compass the city seven times, and the priests shall blow with the trumpets.

Joshua 6:6 - And Joshua the son of Nun called the priests, and said unto them, Take up the ark of the covenant, and let seven priests bear seven trumpets of rams' horns before the ark of the Lord.

Joshua 6:8 - And it came to pass, when Joshua had spoken unto the people, that the seven priests bearing the seven trumpets of rams' horns passed on before the Lord, and blew with the trumpets: and the ark of the covenant of the Lord followed them.

Joshua 6:13 - And seven priests bearing seven trumpets of rams' horns before the ark of the Lord went on continually, and blew with the trumpets: and the armed men went before them; but the armed men came after the ark of the Lord, the priests going on, and blowing with the trumpets.

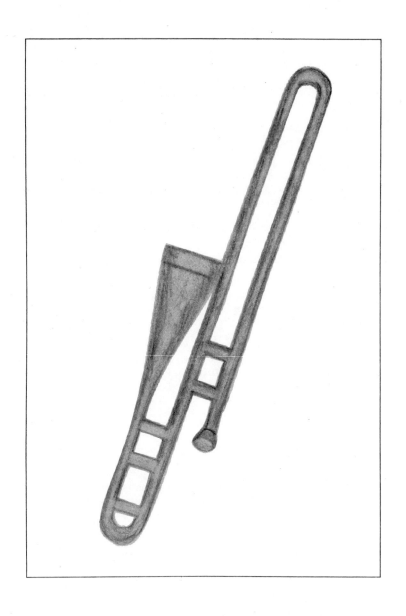

sackbut

The mediaeval precursor of our trombone was called a sackbut, and the term appears in the Biblical book of Daniel. The early sackbut was similar to a trumpet, with a slide mechanism to produce different pitches. The sackbut had a conservatively sized bell, thus producing a rather soft, delicate sound in contrast to today's occasionally bombastic sounding trombone in bands and orchestras.

Daniel 3:5 - That at what time ye hear the sound of the cornet, flute, harp, sackbut, psaltery, dulcimer, and all kinds of musick, ye fall down and worship the golden image that Nebuchadnezzar the king hath set up:

Daniel 3:7 - Therefore at that time, when all the people heard the sound of the cornet, flute, harp, sackbut, psaltery, and all kinds of musick, all the people, the nations, and the languages, fell down and worshipped the golden image that Nebuchadnezzar the king had set up.

Daniel 3:10 - Thou, O king, hast made a decree, that every man that shall hear the sound of the cornet, flute, harp, sackbut, psaltery, and dulcimer, and all kinds of musick, shall fall down and worship the golden image:

Daniel 3:15 - Now if ye be ready that at what time ye hear the sound of the cornet, flute, harp, sackbut, psaltery, and dulcimer, and all kinds of musick, ye fall down and worship the image which I have made; well: but if ye worship not, ye shall be cast the same hour into the midst of a burning fiery furnace; and who is that God that shall deliver you out of my hands?

66

<u>sang</u>

Following is the first of several terms having to do with the human voice as a musical instrument. Significantly, a large proportion of the Biblical musical references herein do indeed refer to the most basic avenue for musical rendition--singing. In a few instances, references are generic in nature, meaning to express rather than to make music. Based on the many entries that follow, it is apparent that singing as an art form has been in existence for many centuries, and that such expression can certainly be used to glorify God.

Exodus 15:1 - Then <u>sang</u> Moses and the children of Israel this song unto the Lord, and spake, saying, I will sing unto the Lord, for he hath triumphed gloriously: the horse and his rider hath he thrown into the sea.

Numbers 21:17 - Then Israel <u>sang</u> this song, Spring up, O well; sing ye unto it:

Judges 5:1 - Then <u>sang</u> Deborah and Barak the son of Abinoam on that day, saying,

I Samuel 29:5 - Is not this David, of whom they <u>sang</u> one to another in dances, saying, Saul slew his thousands, and David his ten thousands?

II Chronicles 29:28 - And all the congregation worshipped, and the singers <u>sang</u>, and the trumpeters sounded: and all this continued until the burnt offering was finished.

II Chronicles 29:30 - Moreover Hezekiah the king and the princes commanded the Levites to sing praise unto the Lord with the words of David, and of Asaph the seer. And they <u>sang</u> praises with gladness, and they bowed their heads and worshipped.

Ezra 3:11 - And they <u>sang</u> together by course in praising and giving thanks unto the Lord; because he is good, for his mercy endureth for ever toward Israel. And all the people shouted with a great shout, when they praised the Lord, because the foundation of the house of the Lord was laid.

Nehemiah 12:42 - And Maaseiah, and Shemaiah, and Eleazar, and Uzzi, and Jehohanan, and Malchijah, and Elam, and Ezer. And the singers <u>sang</u> loud, with Jezrahiah their overseer.

Job 38:7 - When the morning stars <u>sang</u> together, and all the sons of God shouted for joy?

Psalm 7 (heading) - Shiggalon of David, which he <u>sang</u> unto the Lord, concerning the words of Cush the Benjamite.

Psalm 106:12 - Then believed they his words; they <u>sang</u> his praise.

Acts 16:25 - And at midnight Paul and Silas prayed, and <u>sang</u> praises unto God: and the prisoners heard them.

sing

Exodus 15:1 - Then sang Moses and the children of Israel this song unto the Lord, and spake, saying, I will <u>sing</u> unto the Lord, for he hath triumphed gloriously: the horse and his rider hath he thrown into the sea.

Exodus 15:21 - And Miriam answered them, <u>Sing</u> ye to the Lord, for he hath triumphed gloriously; the horse and his rider hath he thrown into the sea.

Exodus 32:18 - And he said, It is not the voice of them that shout for mastery, neither is it the voice of them that cry for being overcome: but the noise of them that <u>sing</u> do I hear.

Numbers 21:17 - Then Israel sang this song, Spring up, O well; <u>sing</u> ye unto it:

Judges 5:3 - Hear, O ye kings; give ear, O ye princes; I, even I, will <u>sing</u> unto the Lord; I will <u>sing</u> praise to the Lord God of Israel.

I Samuel 21:11 - And the servants of Achish said unto him, Is not this David the king of the land? did they not <u>sing</u> one to another of him in dances, saying, Saul hath slain his thousands, and David his ten thousands?

II Samuel 22:50 - Therefore I will give thanks unto thee, O Lord, among the heathen, and I will <u>sing</u> praises unto thy name.

I Chronicles 16:9 - <u>Sing</u> unto him, <u>sing</u> psalms unto him, talk ye of all his wondrous works.

I Chronicles 16:23 - <u>Sing</u> unto the Lord, all the earth; shew forth from day to day his salvation.

I Chronicles 16:33 - Then shall the trees of the wood <u>sing</u> out at the presence of the Lord, because he cometh to judge the earth.

II Chronicles 20:22 - And when they began to <u>sing</u> and to praise, the Lord set ambushments against the children of Ammon, Moab, and mount Seir, which were come against Judah; and they were smitten.

II Chronicles 23:13 - And she looked, and, behold, the king stood at his pillar at the entering in, and the princes and the trumpets by the king: and all the people of the land rejoiced, and sounded with trumpets, also the singers with instruments of musick, and such as taught to <u>sing</u> praise. Then Athaliah rent her clothes,and said, Treason, Treason.

II Chronicles 29:30 - Moreover Hezekiah the king and the princes commanded the Levites to <u>sing</u> praise unto the Lord with the words of David, and of Asaph the seer. And they sang praises with gladness, and they bowed their heads and worshipped.

Job 29:13 - The blessing of him that was ready to perish came upon me: and I caused the widow's heart to <u>sing</u> for joy.

Psalm 7:17 - I will praise the Lord according to his righteousness: and will <u>sing</u> praise to the name of the Lord most high.

Psalm 9:2 - I will be glad to rejoice in thee: I will <u>sing</u> praise to thy name, O thou most High.

Psalm 9:11 - <u>Sing</u> praises to the Lord, which dwelleth in Zion: declare among the people his doings.

Psalm 13:6 - I will <u>sing</u> unto the Lord, because he hath dealt bountifully with me.

Psalm 18:49 - Therefore will I give thanks unto thee, O Lord,among the heathen, and <u>sing</u> praises unto thy name.

Psalm 21:13 - Be thou exalted, Lord, in thine own strength: so will we <u>sing</u> and praise thy power.

Psalm 27:6 - And now shall mine head be lifted up above mine enemies round about me: therefore will I offer in his tabernacle sacrifices of joy: I will <u>sing</u>, yea, I will <u>sing</u> praises unto the Lord.

Psalm 30:4 - <u>Sing</u> unto the Lord, O ye saints of his, and give thanks at the remembrance of his holiness.

Psalm 30:12 - To the end that my glory may <u>sing</u> praise to thee, and not be silent. O Lord my God, I will give thanks unto thee for ever.

Psalm 33:3 - <u>Sing</u> unto him a new song; play skilfully with a loud noise.

Psalm 47:6 - <u>Sing</u> praises to God, <u>sing</u> praises: <u>sing</u> praises unto our King, <u>sing</u> praises.

Psalm 47:7 - For God is the King of all the earth: <u>sing</u> ye praises with understanding.

Psalm 51:14 - Deliver me from bloodguiltiness, O God, thou God of my salvation: and my tongue shall <u>sing</u> aloud of thy righteousness.

Psalm 57:7 - My heart is fixed, O God, my heart is fixed: I will <u>sing</u> and give praise.

Psalm 57:9 - I will praise thee, O Lord, among the people: I will <u>sing</u> unto thee among the nations.

Psalm 59:16 - But I will <u>sing</u> of thy power; yea, I will <u>sing</u> aloud of thy mercy in the morning: for thou hast been my defence and refuge in the day of my trouble.

Psalm 59:17 - Unto thee, O my strength, will I <u>sing</u>: for God is my defence, and the God of my mercy.

Psalm 61:8 - So will I <u>sing</u> praise unto thy name for ever, that I may daily perform my vows.

Psalm 65:13 - The pastures are clothed with flocks; the valleys also are covered over with corn; they shout for joy, they also <u>sing</u>.

Psalm 66:2 - <u>Sing</u> forth the honour of his name: make his praise glorious.

Psalm 66:4 - All the earth shall worship thee, and shall <u>sing</u> unto thee; they shall <u>sing</u> to thy name. Selah.

Psalm 67:4 - O let the nations be glad and <u>sing</u> for joy: for thou shalt judge the people righteously, and govern the nations upon earth. Selah.

Psalm 68:32 - <u>Sing</u> unto God, ye kingdoms of the earth; O <u>sing</u> praises unto the Lord; Selah:

Psalm 71:22 - I will also praise thee with the psaltery, even thy truth, O my God: unto thee will I <u>sing</u> with the harp, O thou Holy One of Israel.

Psalm 71:23 - My lips shall greatly rejoice when I <u>sing</u> unto thee; and my soul, which thou hast redeemed.

Psalm 75:9 - But I will declare for ever; I will <u>sing</u> praises to the God of Jacob.

Psalm 81:1 - <u>Sing</u> aloud unto God our strength: make a joyful noise unto the God of Jacob.

Psalm 89:1 - I will <u>sing</u> of the mercies of the Lord for ever: with my mouth will I make known thy faithfulness to all generations.

Psalm 92:1 - It is a good thing to give thanks unto the Lord, and to <u>sing</u> praises unto thy name, O Most High:

Psalm 95:1 - O come, let us <u>sing</u> unto the Lord: let us make a joyful noise to the rock of our salvation.

Psalm 96:1 - O <u>sing</u> unto the Lord a new song: <u>sing</u> unto the Lord, all the earth.

Psalm 96:2 - <u>Sing</u> unto the Lord, bless his name; shew forth his salvation from day to day.

Psalm 98:1 - O <u>sing</u> unto the Lord a new song; for he hath done marvellous things: his right hand, and his holy arm, hath gotten him the victory.

Psalm 98:4 - Make a joyful noise unto the Lord, all the earth: make a loud noise, and rejoice, and sing praise.

Psalm 98:5 - Sing unto the Lord with the harp; with the harp, and the voice of a psalm.

Psalm 101:1 - I will sing of mercy and judgment: unto thee, O Lord, will I sing.

Psalm 104:12 - By them shall the fowls of the heaven have their habitation, which sing among the branches.

Psalm 104:33 - I will sing unto the Lord as long as I live: I will sing praise to my God while I have my being.

Psalm 105:2 - Sing unto him, sing psalms unto him: talk ye of all his wondrous works.

Psalm 108:1 - O God, my heart is fixed; I will sing and give praise, even with my glory.

Psalm 108:3 - I will praise thee, O Lord, among the people: and I will sing praises unto thee among the nations.

Psalm 135:3 - praise the Lord; for the Lord is good: sing praises unto his name; for it is pleasant.

Psalm 137:3 - For there they that carried us away captive required of us a song; and they that wasted us required of us mirth, saying, Sing us one of the songs of Zion.

Psalm 137:4 - How shall we sing the Lord's song in a strange land?

Psalm 138:1 - I will praise thee with my whole heart: before the gods will I sing praise unto thee.

Psalm 138:5 - Yea, they shall sing in the ways of the Lord: for great is the glory of the Lord.

Psalm 144:9 - I will sing a new song unto thee, O God: upon a psaltery and an instrument of ten strings will I sing praises unto thee.

Psalm 145:7 - They shall abundantly utter the memory of thy great goodness, and shall sing of thy righteousness.

Psalm 146:2 - While I live will I praise the Lord: I will sing praises unto my God while I have my being.

Psalm 147:1 - Praise ye the Lord: for it is good to sing praises unto our God; for it is pleasant; and praise is comely.

Psalm 147:7 - <u>Sing</u> unto the Lord with thanksgiving; <u>sing</u> praise upon the harp unto our God:

Psalm 149:1 - Praise ye the Lord. <u>Sing</u> unto the Lord a new song, and his praise in the congregation of saints.

Psalm 149:3 - Let them praise his name in the dance: let them <u>sing</u> praises unto him with the timbrel and harp.

Psalm 149:5 - Let the saints be joyful in glory: let them <u>sing</u> aloud upon their beds.

Proverbs 29:6 - In the transgression of an evil man there is a snare: but the righteous doth <u>sing</u> and rejoice.

Isaiah 5:1 - Now will I <u>sing</u> to my well-beloved a song of my beloved touching his vineyard. My well-beloved hath a vineyard in a very fruitful hill:

Isaiah 12:5 - <u>Sing</u> unto the Lord; for he hath done excellent things: this is known in all the earth.

Isaiah 23:15 - And it shall come to pass in that day, that Tyre shall be forgotten seventy years, according to the days of one king: after the end of seventy years shall Tyre <u>sing</u> as an harlot.

Isaiah 23:16 - Take an harp, go about the city, thou harlot that hast been forgotten; make sweet melody, <u>sing</u> many songs, that thou mayest be remembered.

Isaiah 24:14 - They shall lift up their voice, they shall <u>sing</u> for the majesty of the Lord, they shall cry aloud from the sea.

Isaiah 26:19 - Thy dead men shall live, together with my dead body shall they arise. Awake and <u>sing</u>, ye that dwell in dust: for thy dew is as the dew of herbs, and the earth shall cast out the dead.

Isaiah 27:2 - In that day <u>sing</u> ye unto her, A vineyard of red wine.

Isaiah 35:6 - Then shall the lame man leap as an hart, and the tongue of the dumb <u>sing</u>: for in the wilderness shall waters break out, and streams in the desert.

Isaiah 38:20 - The Lord was ready to save me: therefore we will <u>sing</u> my songs to the stringed instruments all the days of our life in the house of the Lord.

Isaiah 42:10 - <u>Sing</u> unto the Lord a new song, and his praise from the end of the earth, ye that go down to the sea, and all that is therein; the isles, and the inhabitants thereof.

Isaiah 42:11 - Let the wilderness and the cities thereof lift up their voice, the villages that Kedar doth inhabit: let the inhabitants of the rock sing, let them shout from the top of the mountains.

Isaiah 44:23 - Sing, O ye heavens; for the Lord hath done it: shout, ye lower parts of the earth: break forth into singing, ye mountains, O forest, and every tree therein: for the Lord hath redeemed Jacob, and glorified himself in Israel.

Isaiah 49:13 - Sing, O heavens; and be joyful, O earth; and break forth into singing, O mountains: for the Lord hath comforted his people, and will have mercy upon his afflicted.

Isaiah 52:8 - Thy watchmen shall lift up the voice; with the voice together shall they sing: for they shall see eye to eye, when the Lord shall bring again Zion.

Isaiah 52:9 - Break forth into joy, sing together, ye waste places of Jerusalem: for the Lord hath comforted his people, he hath redeemed Jerusalem.

Isaiah 54:1 - Sing, O barren, thou that didst not bear; break forth into singing, and cry aloud, thou that didst not travail with child: for more are the children of the desolate than the children of the married wife, saith the Lord.

Isaiah 54:14 - Behold, my servants shall sing for joy of heart, but ye shall cry for sorrow of heart, and shall howl for vexation of spirit.

Jeremiah 20:13 - Sing unto the Lord, praise ye the Lord: for he hath delivered the soul of the poor from the hand of evildoers.

Jeremiah 31:7 - For thus saith the Lord; Sing with gladness for Jacob, and shout among the chief of the nations: publish ye, praise ye, and say, O Lord, save thy people, the remnant of Israel.

Jeremiah 31:12 - Therefore they shall come and sing in the height of Zion, and shall flow together to the goodness of the Lord, for wheat, and for wine, and for oil, and for the young of the flock and of the herd: and their soul shall be as a watered garden; and they shall not sorrow any more at all.

Jeremiah 51:48 - Then the heaven and the earth, and all that is therein, shall sing for Babylon: for the spoilers shall come unto her from the north, saith the Lord.

Ezekiel 27:25 - The ships of Tarshish did sing of thee in thy market: and thou wast replenished, and made very glorious in the midst of the seas.

Hosea 2:15 - And I will give her her vineyards from thence, and the valley of Achor for a door of hope: and she shall sing there, as in the days of her youth, and as in the day when she came up out of the land of Egypt.

Zephaniah 2:14 - And flocks shall lie down in the midst of her, all the beasts of the nations: both the cormorant and the bittern shall lodge in the upper lintels of it; their voice shall sing in the windows; desolation shall be in the thresholds: for he shall uncover the cedar work.

Zephaniah 3:14 - Sing, O daughter of Zion; shout, O Israel; be glad and rejoice with all the heart, O daughter of Jerusalem.

Zechariah 2:10 - Sing and rejoice, O daughter of Zion: for lo, I come, and I will dwell in the midst of thee, saith the Lord.

Romans 15:9 - And that the Gentiles might glorify God for his mercy; as it is written, For this cause I will confess to thee among the Gentiles, and sing unto thy name.

I Corinthians 14:15 - What is it then? I will pray with the spirit, and I will pray with the understanding also: I will sing with the spirit, and I will sing with the understanding also.

Hebrews 2:12 - Saying, I will declare thy name unto thy brethren, in the midst of the church will I sing praise unto thee.

James 5:13 - Is any among you afflicted? let him pray. Is any merry? let him sing psalms.

Revelation 15:3 - And they sing the song of Moses the servant of God, and the song of the Lamb, saying, Great and marvellous are thy works, Lord God Almighty; just and true are thy ways, thou King of saints.

singer(s)

In the professional music world of the 20th Century, "singers" and "musicians" are sometimes referred to as separate entities, often in a rather sarcastic manner--perhaps relating to the previously mentioned tendency of vocalists to emotionalize and concurrently to not intellectualize, or count rhythms, to name a specific task of the general musician. Clearly, Scriptural references to singers do not set a precedent for this attitude, instead incorporating the terms "singers" and "musicians" as a single concept involving use of the human body and talent to produce music of the soul in the worship of God.

I Kings 10:12 - And the king made of the almug trees pillars for the house of the Lord, and for the king's house, harps also and psalteries for singers: there came no such almug trees, nor were seen unto this day.

I Chronicles 6:33 - And these are they that waited with their children. Of the sons of the Kohathites: Heman a singer, the son of Joel, the son of Shemuel,

I Chronicles 9:33 - And these are the singers, chief of the fathers of the Levites, who remaining in the chambers were free: for they were employed in that work day and night.

I Chronicles 15:16 - And David spake to the chief of the Levites to appoint their brethren to be the singers with instruments of musick, psalteries and harps and cymbals, sounding, by lifting up the voice with joy.

I Chronicles 15:19 - So the singers, Heman, Asaph, and Ethan, were appointed to sound with cymbals of brass;

I Chronicles 15:27 - And David was clothed with a robe of fine linen, and all the Levites that bare the ark, and the singers, and Chenaniah the master of the song with the singers: David also had upon him an ephod of linen.

II Chronicles 5:12 - Also the Levites which were the singers, all of them of Asaph, of Heman, of Jeduthun, with their sons and their brethren, being arrayed in white linen, having cymbals and psalteries and harps, stood at the east end of the altar, and with them an hundred and twenty priests sounding with trumpets:)

I Chronicles 5:13 - It came even to pass, as the trumpeters and singers were as one, to make one sound to be heard in praising and thanking the Lord; and when they lifted up their voice with the trumpets and cymbals and instruments of musick, and praised the Lord, saying, For he is good; for his mercy endureth forever: that then the house was filled with a cloud, even the house of the Lord;

II Chronicles 9:11 - And the king made of the algum trees terraces to the house of the Lord, and to the king's palace, and harps and psalteries for singers: and there were none such seen before in the land of Judah.

II Chronicles 20:21 - And when he had consulted with the people, he appointed singers unto the Lord, and that should praise the beauty of holiness, as they went out before the army, and to say, Praise the Lord; for his mercy endureth for ever.

II Chronicles 23:13 - And she looked, and, behold, the king stood at his pillar at the entering in, and the princes and the trumpets by the king: and all the people of the land rejoiced, and sounded with trumpets, also the singers with instruments of musick, and such as taught to sing praise. Then Athaliah rent her clothes, and said, Treason, Treason.

II Chronicles 29:28 - And all the congregation worshipped, and the singers sang, and the trumpeters sounded: and all this continued until the burnt offering was finished.

II Chronicles 35:14 - And the singers the sons of Asaph were in their place, according to the commandment of David, and Asaph, and Heman, and Jeduthun the king's seer; and the porters waited at every gate; they might not depart from their service; for their brethren the Levites prepared for them.

Ezra 2:41 - The singers: the children of Asaph, an hundred twenty and eight.

Ezra 2:70 - So the priests, and the Levites, and some of the people, and the singers, and the porters, and the Hethinims, dwelt in their cities, and all Israel in their cities.

Ezra 7:7 - And there went up some of the children of Israel, and of the priests, and the Levites, and the singers, and the porters, and the Nethinims, unto Jerusalem, in the seventh year of Artaxerxes the king.

Ezra 7:24 - Also we certify you, that touching any of the priests and Levites, singers, porters, Nethinims, or ministers of this house of God, it shall not be lawful to impose toll, tribute, or custom, upon them.

Ezra 10:24 - Of the singers also; Eliashib: and of the porters; Shallum, and Telem, and Uri.

Nehemiah 7:1 - Now it came to pass, when the wall was built, and I had set up the doors, and the porters and the singers and the Levites were appointed,

Nehemiah 7:44 - The <u>singers</u>: the children of Asaph, an hundred forty and eight.

Nehemiah 7:73 - So the priests, and the Levites, and the porters, and the <u>singers</u>, and some of the people, and the Nethinims, and all Israel, dwelt in their cities; and when the seventh month came, the children of Israel were in their cities.

Nehemiah 10:28 - And the rest of the people, the priests, the Levites, the porters, the <u>singers</u>, the Nethinims, and all they that had separated themselves from the people of the lands unto the law of God, their wives, their sons, and their daughters, every one having knowledge, and having understanding;

Nehemiah 10:39 - For the children of Israel and the children of Levi shall bring the offering of the corn, of the new wine, and the oil, unto the chambers, where are the vessels of the sanctuary, and the priests that minister, and the porters, and the <u>singers</u>: and we will not forsake the house of our God.

Nehemiah 11:22 - The overseer also of the Levites at Jerusalem was Uzzi the son of Bani, the son of Hashabiah, the son of Mattaniah, the son of Micha. Of the sons of Asaph, the <u>singers</u> were over the business of the house of God.

Nehemiah 11:23 - For it was the king's commandment concerning them, that a certain portion should be for the <u>singers</u>, due for every day.

Nehemiah 12:28 - And the sons of the <u>singers</u> gathered themselves together, both out of the plain country round about Jerusalem, and from the villages of Netophathi;

Nehemiah 12:29 - Also from the house of Gilgal, and out of the fields of Geba and Azmaveth: for the <u>singers</u> had builded them villages round about Jerusalem.

Nehemiah 12:42 - And Maaseiah, and Shemaiah, and Eleazar, and Uzzi, and Jehohanan, and Malchijah, and Elam, and Ezer. And the <u>singers</u> sang loud, with Jezrahiah their overseer.

Nehemiah 12:45 - And both the <u>singers</u> and the porters kept the ward of their God, and the ward of the purification, according to the commandment of David, and of Solomon his son.

Nehemiah 12:46 - For in the days of David and Asaph of old there were chief of the <u>singers</u>, and songs of praise and thanksgiving unto God.

Nehemiah 12:47 - And all Israel in the days of Zerubbabel, and in the days of Nehemiah, gave the portions of the <u>singers</u> and the porters, every day his portion: and they sanctified holy things unto the Levites; and the Levites sanctified them unto the children of Aaron.

78

Nehemiah 13:5 - and he had prepared for him a great chamber, where aforetime they laid the meat offerings, the frankincense, and the vessels, and the tithes of the corn, the new wine, and the oil, which was commanded to be given to the Levites, and the <u>singers</u>, and the porters; and the offerings of the priests.

Nehemiah 13:10 - And I perceived that the portions of the Levites had not been given them: for the Levites and the <u>singers</u>, that did the work, were fled every one to his field.

Psalm 68:25 - The <u>singers</u> went before, the players on instruments followed after; among them were the damsels playing with timbrels.

Psalm 87:7 - As well the <u>singers</u> as the payers on instruments shall be there: all my springs are in thee.

Ecclesiastes 2:8 - I gathered me also silver and gold,and the peculiar treasure of kings and of the provinces: I gat me men <u>singers</u> and women <u>singers</u>, and the delights of the sons of men, as musical instruments, and that of all sorts.

Ezekiel 40:44 - And without the inner gate were the chambers of the <u>singers</u> in the inner court, which was at the side of the north gate; and their prospect was toward the south: one at the side of the east gate having the prospect toward the north.

Habakkuk 3:19 - The Lord God is my strength, and he will make me feel like hinds' feet, and he will make me to walk upon mine high places. To the chief <u>singer</u> on my stringed instruments.

singeth

Proverbs 25:20 - As he that taketh away a garment in cold weather, and as vinegar upon nitre, so is he that <u>singeth</u> songs to an heavy heart.

singing

I Samuel 18:6 - And it came to pass as they came, when David was returned from the slaughter of the Philistine, that the women came out of all cities of Israel, <u>singing</u> and dancing, to meet king Saul, with tabrets, with joy, and with instruments of musick.

II Samuel 19:35 - I am this day fourscore years old: and I can discern between good and evil? can thy servant taste what I eat or what I drink? can I hear any more the voice of <u>singing</u> men and <u>singing</u> women? wherefore then should thy servant be yet a burden unto my lord the king?

I Chronicles 6:32 - And they ministered before the dwelling place of the tabernacle of the congregation with singing, until Solomon had built the house of the Lord in Jerusalem: and then they waited on their office according to their order.

I Chronicles 13:8 - And David and all Israel played before God with all their might, and with singing, and with harps, and with psalteries, and with timbrels, and with cymbals, and with trumpets.

II Chronicles 23:18 - Also Jehoiada appointed the offices of the house of the Lord by the hand of the priests the Levites, whom David had distributed in the house of the Lord, to offer the burnt offerings of the Lord, as it is written in the law of Moses, with rejoicing and with singing, as it was ordained by David.

II Chronicles 30:21 - And the children of Israel that were present at Jerusalem kept the feast of unleavened bread seven days with great gladness: and the Levites and the priests praised the Lord day by day, singing with loud instruments unto the Lord.

II Chronicles 35:25 - And Jeremiah lamented for Josiah: and all the singing men and the singing women spake of Josiah in their lamentations to this day, and made them an ordinance in Israel: and, behold, they are written in the lamentations.

Ezra 2:65 - Beside their servants and their maids, of whom there were seven thousand three hundred thirty and seven: and there were among them two hundred singing men and singing women.

Nehemiah 7:67 - Beside their manservants and their maidservants, of whom there were seven thousand three hundred thirty and seven: and they had two hundred forty and five singing men and singing women.

Nehemiah 12:27 - And at the dedication of the wall of Jerusalem they sought the Levites out of all their places, to bring them to Jerusalem, to keep the dedication with gladness, both with thanksgivings, and with singing, with cymbals, psalteries, and with harps.

Psalm 100:2 - Serve the Lord with gladness: come before his presence with singing.

Psalm 126:2 - Then was our mouth filled with laughter, and our tongue with singing: then said they among the heathen, The Lord hath done great things for them.

Song of Solomon 2:12 - The flowers appear on the earth; the time of the singing of birds is come, and the voice of the turtle is heard in our land;

Isaiah 14:7 - The whole earth is at rest, and is quiet: they break forth into singing.

Isaiah 16:10 - And gladness is taken away, and joy out of the plentiful field; and in the vineyards there shall be no singing, neither shall there be shouting: the treaders shall tread out no wine in their presses; I have made their vintage shouting to cease.

Isaiah 35:2 - It shall blossom abundantly, and rejoice even with joy and singing: the glory of Lebanon shall be given unto it, the excellency of Carmel and Sharon, they shall see the glory of the Lord, and the excellency of our God.

Isaiah 44:23 - Sing, O ye heavens; for the Lord heath done it: shout, ye lower parts of the earth: break forth into singing, ye mountains, O forest, and every tree therein: for the Lord hath redeemed Jacob, and glorified himself in Israel.

Isaiah 48:20 - Go ye forth of Babylon, flee ye from the Chaldeans, with a voice of singing declare ye, tell this, utter it even to the end of the earth; say ye, The Lord hath redeemed his servant Jacob.

Isaiah 49:13 - Sing, O heavens; and be joyful, O earth; and break forth into singing, O mountains: for the Lord hath comforted his people, and will have mercy upon his afflicted.

Isaiah 51:11 - Therefore the redeemed of the Lord shall return, and come with singing unto Zion; and everlasting joy shall be upon their head: they shall obtain gladness and joy; and sorrow and mourning shall flee away.

Isaiah 54:1 - Sing, O barren, thou that didst not bear; break forth into singing, and cry aloud, thou that didst not travail with child: for more are the children of the desolate than the children of the married wife, saith the Lord.

Isaiah 55:12 - For ye shall go out with joy, and be led forth with peace: the mountains and the hills shall break forth before you into singing, and all the trees of the field shall clap their hands.

Zephaniah 3:17 - The Lord thy God in the midst of thee is mighty; he will save, he will rejoice over thee with joy; he will rest in his love, he will joy over thee with singing.

Ephesians 5:19 - Speaking to yourselves in psalms and hymns and spiritual songs, singing and making melody in your heart to the Lord;

Colossians 3:16 - Let the word of Christ dwell in you richly in all wisdom; teaching and admonishing one another in psalms and hymns and spiritual songs, singing with grace in your hearts to the Lord.

song (Song)

This collection of Scriptural references to the word "song" probably contains the most-often-quoted passages in this book, especially in sacred choral music of the 20th Century. Phrases such as "Sing to the Lord a new song" and "The Lord is my strength and song" have served contemporary composers many times as inspiration for words and music. This particular listing also includes the fifteen headings of the "songs of ascents" or "songs of degrees," the Psalms 120 through 134 which were sung by Hebrew pilgrims while journeying to Jerusalem.

Of course the standard definition of "song" is a melody set to words. Broadly speaking, a song can be any lyrical musical statement, as in the case of a bird's song, or Felix Mendelssohn's "Songs without Words" for solo piano. The many references herein offer a good idea of the high opinion held by Biblical writers for a song of beauty, and perhaps a hint of the surprising variation in musical styles that apparently existed many hundreds of years ago.

Exodus 15:1 - Then sang Moses and the children of Israel this song unto the Lord, and spake, saying, I will sing unto the Lord, for he hath triumphed gloriously: the horse and his rider hath he thrown into the sea.

Exodus 15:2 - The Lord is my strength and song, and he is become my salvation: he is my God, and I will prepare him an habitation; my father's God, and I will exalt him.

Numbers 21:17 - Then Israel sang this song, Spring up, O well; sing ye unto it:

Deuteronomy 31:19 - Now therefore write ye this song for you, and teach it the children of Israel: put it in their mouths, that this song may be witness for me against the children of Israel.

Deuteronomy 31:21 - And it shall come to pass, when many evils and troubles are befallen them, that this song shall testify against them as a witness; for it shall not be forgotten out of the mouths of their seed: for I know their imagination which they go about, even now, before I have brought them into the land which I sware.

Deuteronomy 31:22 - Moses therefore wrote this song the same day, and taught it the children of Israel.

Deuteronomy 31:30 - And Moses spake in the ears of all the congregation of Israel the words of this song, until they were ended.

Deuteronomy 32:44 - And Moses came and spake all the words of this song in the ears of the people, he, and Hoshea the son of Nun.

Judges 5:12 - Awake, awake, Deborah: awake, awake, utter a song: arise, Barak, and lead thy captivity captive, thou son of Abinoam.

II Samuel 22:1 - And David spake unto the Lord the words of this song in the day that the Lord had delivered him out of the hand of all his enemies, and out of the hand of Saul:

I Chronicles 6:31 - And these are they whom David set over the service of song in the house of the Lord, after that the ark had rest.

I Chronicles 15:22 - And Chenaniah, chief of the Levites, was for song: he instructed about the song, because he was skilful.

I Chronicles 15:27 - And David was clothed with a robe of fine linen, and all the Levites that bare the ark, and the singers, and Chenaniah the master of the song with the singers: David also had upon him an ephod of linen.

I Chronicles 25:6 - All these were under the hands of their father for song in the house of the Lord, with cymbals, psalteries, and harps, for the service of the house of God, according to the king's order to Asaph, Jeduthun, and Heman.

II Chronicles 29:27 - And Hezekiah commanded to offer the burnt offering upon the altar. And when the burnt offering began, the song of the Lord began also with the trumpets, and with the instruments ordained by David king of Israel.

Job 30:9 - And now am I their song, yea, I am their byword.

Psalm 18 (heading) - To the chief Musician, A Psalm of David, the servant of the Lord, who spake unto the Lord the words of this song in the day that the Lord delivered him from the hand of all his enemies, and from the hand of Saul: And he said,

Psalm 28:7 - The Lord is my strength and my shield; my heart trusted in him, and I am helped: therefore my heart greatly rejoiceth; and with my song will I praise him.

Psalm 30 (heading) - A Psalm and Song at the dedication of the house of David.

Psalm 33:3 - Sing unto him a new song; play skilfully with a loud noise.

Psalm 40:3 - And he hath put a new song in my mouth, even praise unto our God: many shall see it, and fear, and shall trust in the Lord.

Psalm 42:8 - Yet the Lord will command his lovingkindness in the daytime, and in the night his song shall be with me, and my prayer unto the God of my life.

Psalm 45 (heading) - To the chief Musician upon Shoshannim, for the sons of Korah, Maschil, A Song of loves.

Psalm 46 (heading) - To the chief Musician for the sons of Korah, A Song upon Alamoth.

Psalm 48 (heading) - A Song and Psalm for the sons of Korah.

Psalm 65 (heading) - To the chief Musician, A Psalm and Song of David.

Psalm 66 (heading) - To the chief Musician, A Song or Psalm.

Psalm 67 (heading) - To the chief Musician, A Psalm or Song.

Psalm 68 (heading) - To the chief Musician, A Psalm or Song of David.

Psalm 69:12 - They that sit in the gate speak aginst me; and I was the song of the drunkards.

Psalm 69:30 - I will praise the name of God with a song, and will magnify him with thanksgiving.

Psalm 75 (heading) - To the chief Musician, Al-taschith, A Psalm or Song of Asaph.

Psalm 76 (heading) - To the chief Musician on Neginoth, A Psalm or Song of Asaph.

Psalm 77:6 - I call to remembrance my song in the night: I commune with mine own heart: and my spirit made diligent search.

Psalm 83 (heading) - A Song or Psalm of Asaph.

Psalm 87 (heading) - A Psalm or Song for the sons of Korah.

Psalm 88 (heading) - A Song or Psalm for the sons of Korah, to the chief Musician upon Mahalath Leannoth, Maschil of Heman the Ezrahite.

Psalm 92 (heading) - A Psalm or Song for the sabbath day.

Psalm 96:1 - O sing unto the Lord a new song: sing unto the Lord, all the earth.

Psalm 98:1 - O sing unto the Lord a new song; for he hath done marvellous things: his right hand, and his holy arm, hath gotten him the victory.

Psalm 108 (heading) - A Song or Psalm of David.

Psalm 118:14 - The Lord is my strength and song, and is become my salvation.

Psalm 120 (heading) - A Song of degrees.

Psalm 121 (heading) - A Song of degrees.

Psalm 122 (heading) - A Song of degrees of David.

Psalm 123 (heading) - A Song of degrees.

Psalm 124 (heading) - A Song of degrees of David.

Psalm 125 (heading) - A Song of degrees.

Psalm 126 (heading) - A Song of degrees.

Psalm 127 (heading) - A Song of degrees for Solomon.

Psalm 128 (heading) - A Song of degrees.

Psalm 129 (heading) - A Song of degrees.

Psalm 130 (heading) - A Song of degrees.

Psalm 131 (heading) - A Song of degrees of David.

Psalm 132 (heading) - A Song of degrees.

Psalm 133 (heading) - A Song of degrees of David.

Psalm 134 (heading) - A Song of degrees.

Psalm 137:3 - For there they that carried us away captive required of us a song; and they that wasted us required of us mirth, saying, Sing us one of the songs of Zion.

Psalm 137:4 - How shall we sing the Lord's song in a strange land?

Psalm 144:9 - I will sing a new song unto thee, O God: upon a psaltery and an instrument of ten strings will I sing praises unto thee.

Psalm 149:1 - Praise ye the Lord. Sing unto the Lord a new song, and his praise in the congregation of saints.

Ecclesiastes 7:5 - It is better to hear the rebuke of the wise, than for a man to hear the song of fools.

Song of Solomon 1:1 - The <u>song</u> of songs, which is Solomon's.

Isaiah 5:1 - Now will I sing to my well-beloved a <u>song</u> of my beloved touching his vineyard. My well-beloved hath a vineyard in a very fruitful hill:

Isaiah 12:2 - Behold, God is my salvation; I will trust, and not be afraid: for the Lord Jehovah is my strength and my <u>song</u>; he also is become my salvation.

Isaiah 24:9 - They shall not drink wine with a <u>song</u>; strong drink shall be bitter to them that drink it.

Isaiah 26:1 - In that day shall this <u>song</u> be sung in the land of Judah; We have a strong city; salvation will God appoint for walls and bulwarks.

Isaiah 30:29 - Ye shall have a <u>song</u>, as in the night when a holy solemnity is kept; and gladness of heart, as when one goeth with a pipe to come into the mountain of the Lord, to the might One of Israel.

Isaiah 42:10 - Sing unto the Lord a new <u>song</u>, and his praise from the end of the earth, ye that go down to the sea, and all that is therein; the isles, and the inhabitants thereof.

Lamentations 3:14 - I was a derision to all my people; and their <u>song</u> all the day.

Ezekiel 33:32 - And, lo, thou art unto them as a very lovely <u>song</u> of one that hath a pleasant voice, and can play well on an instrument: for they hear thy words, but they do them not.

Revelation 5:9 - And they sung a new <u>song</u>, saying, Thou art worthy to take the book, and to open the seals thereof: for thou wast slain, and hast redeemed us to God by thy blood out of every kindred, and tongue, and people, and nation;

Revelation 14:3 - And they sung as it were a new <u>song</u> before the throne, and before the four beasts, and the elders: and no man could learn that <u>song</u> but the hundred and forty and four thousand, which were redeemed from the earth.

Revelation 15:3 - And they sing the <u>song</u> of Moses the servant of God, and the <u>song</u> of the Lamb, saying, Great and marvellous are thy works, Lord God Almighty; just and true are thy ways, thou King of saints.

songs

Genesis 31:27 - Wherefore didst thou flee away secretly, and steal away from me; and didst not tell me, that I might have sent thee away with mirth, and with songs, with tabret, and with harp?

I Kings 4:32 - And he spake three thousand proverbs: and his songs were a thousand and five.

I Chronicles 25:7 - So the number of them, with their brethren that were instructed in the songs of the Lord, even all that were cunning, was two hundred fourscore and eight.

Nehemiah 12:46 - For in the days of David and Asaph of old there were chief of the singers, and songs of praise and thanksgiving unto God.

Job 35:10 - But none saith, Where is God my maker, who giveth songs in the night;

Psalm 32:7 - Thou art my hiding place; thou shalt preserve me from trouble; thou shalt compass me about with songs of deliverance. Selah.

Psalm 119:54 - Thy statues have been my songs in the house of my pilgrimage.

Psalm 137:3 - For there they that carried us away captive required of us a song; and they that wasted us required of us mirth, saying, Sing us one of the songs of Zion.

Proverbs 25:20 - As he that taketh away a garment in cold weather, and as vinegar upon nitre, so is he that singeth songs to an heavy heart.

Song of Solomon 1:1 - The song of songs, which is Solomon's.

Isaiah 23:16 - Take an harp, go about the city, thou harlot that hast been forgotten; make sweet melody, sing many songs, that thou mayest be remembered.

Isaiah 24:16 - From the uttermost part of the earth have we heard songs, even glory to the righteous. But I said, My leanness my leanness, woe unto me! the treacherous dealers have dealt treacherously; yea, the treacherous dealers have dealt very treacherously.

Isaiah 35:10 - And the ransomed of the Lord shall return, and come to Zion with songs and everlasting joy upon their heads: they shall obtain joy and gladness, and sorrow and sighing shall flee away.

Isaiah 38:20 - The Lord was ready to save me: therefore we will sing my songs to the stringed instruments all the days of our life in the house of the Lord.

88

Ezekiel 26:13 - And I will cause the noise of thy <u>songs</u> to cease; and the sound of thy harps shall be no more heard.

Amos 5:23 - Take thou away from me the noise of thy <u>songs</u>; for I will not hear the melody of thy viols.

Amos 8:3 - And the <u>songs</u> of the temple shall be howlings in that day, saith the Lord God: there shall be many dead bodies in every place; they shall cast them forth with silence.

Amos 8:10 - And I will turn your feasts into mourning, and all your <u>songs</u> into lamentation; and I will bring up sackcloth upon all loins, and baldness upon every head; and I will make it as the mourning of an only son, and the end thereof as a bitter day.

Ephesians 5:19 - Speaking to yourselves in psalms and hymns and spiritual <u>songs</u>, singing and making melody in your heart to the Lord;

Colossians 3:16 - Let the word of Christ dwell in you richly in all wisdom; teaching and admonishing one another in psalms and hymns and spiritual <u>songs</u>, singing with grace in your hearts to the Lord.

spiritual songs

It is interesting to note that the major types of religious songs mentioned in the Bible are psalms, hymns, and spiritual songs. In the 20th Century in the Western world, we have come to regard spirituals as a specific type of religious song invented and mastered by black peoples in North America. Broadly speaking, the Scriptural term and the modern term would mean about the same thing--a religious song that is injected with a certain kind of sometimes happy, sometimes melancholy, enthusiasm, or "spirit." The latter 20th-Century musical term "gospel" seems to be an outgrowth of the spiritual song idea, incorporating a sometimes popular, and a sometimes sacred (or religious) flavor in music. The fact that a single type of music could be both sacred and popular is somewhat foreign to the classical-popular music division that is an outgrowth of Western influences over the past few centuries. However, it is nonetheless real: "gospel" or "spiritual" songs can at times be intensely emotional in a religious way--reflecting the sacred, and at other times can be similar to popular or folk music--especially of the commercial variety.

Ephesians 5:19 - Speaking to yourselves in psalms and hymns and spiritual songs, singing and making melody in your heart to the Lord;

Colossians 3:16 - Let the word of Christ dwell in you richly in all wisdom; teaching and admonishing one another in psalms and hymns and spiritual songs, singing with grace in your hearts to the Lord.

sung

Isaiah 26:1 - In that day shall this song be sung in the land of Judah; We have a strong city; salvation will God appoint for walls and bulwarks.

Matthew 26:30 - And when they had sung an hymn, they went out into the mount of Olives.

Mark 14:26 - And when they had sung an hymn, they went out into the Mount of Olives.

Revelation 5:9 - And they <u>sung</u> a new song, saying, Thou art worthy to take the book, and to open the seals thereof: for thou wast slain, and hast redeemed us to God by thy blood out of every kindred, and tongue, and people, and nation;

Revelation 14:3 - And they <u>sung</u> as it were a new song before the throne, and before the four beasts, and the elders: and no man could learn that song but the hundred and forty and four thousand, which were redeemed from the earth.

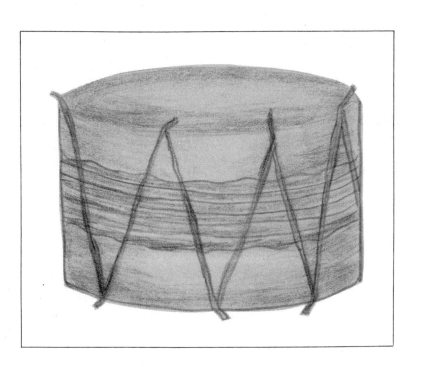

tabret(s)

The tabret of the holy Scriptures is apparently a small drum, perhaps at times played in pairs or groups. I would assume that the tabret was perhaps sounded with the hands, rather than with sticks, although the latter is certainly a possibility. The Scriptural association of mirth with tabrets leads me to suspect that they were rather small and delicate sounding, at any rate.

In a few instances, the tabret is associated with the musical pipe, a simple type of flute. In mediaeval Europe, we know of the "pipe and tabor" played by one person. In this instance, the pipe with a few finger holes was played with one hand, while the tabor--a small drum attached to a "sling" strung around the shoulder--was struck by a mallet or stick held by the other hand. This dual technique is performed in a virtuosic manner by some contemporary artists who specialize in performing resurrected music of mediaeval and Renaissance Europe. The Biblical association of pipe and tabret was perhaps a precursor of the later pipe and tabor.

Genesis 31:37 - Wherefore didst thou flee away secretly, and steal way from me; and didst not tell me, that I might have sent thee away with mirth, and with songs, with tabret, and with harp?

I Samuel 10:5 - After that thou shalt come to the hill of God, where is the garrison of the Philistines: and it shall come to pass, when thou art come thither to the city, that thou shalt meet a company of prophets coming down from the high place with a psaltery, and a tabret, and a pipe, and a harp before them; and they shall prophesy:

I Samuel 18:6 - And it came to pass as they came, when David was returned from the slaughter of the Philistine, that the women came out of all cities of Israel, singing and dancing, to meet king Saul, with tabrets, with joy, and with instruments of musick.

Job 17:6 - He hath made me also a byword of the people; and aforetime I was as a tabret.

Isaiah 5:12 - And the harp, and the viol, the tabret, and pipe, and wine, are in their feasts: but they regard not the work of the Lord, neither consider the operation of his hands.

Isaiah 24:8 - The mirth of tabrets ceaseth, the noise of them that rejoice endeth, the joy of the harp ceaseth.

Isaiah 30:32 - And in every place where the grounded staff shall pass, which the Lord shall lay upon him, it shall be with tabrets and harps: and in battles of shaking will he fight with it.

Jeremiah 31:4 - Again I will build thee, and thou shalt be built, O virgin of Israel: thou shalt again be adorned with thy tabrets, and shalt go forth in the dances of them that make merry.

Ezekiel 28:13 - Thou hast been in Eden the garden of God; every previous stone was thy covering, the sardius, topaz, and the diamond, the beryl, the onyx, and the jasper, the sapphire, the emerald, and the carbuncle, and gold: the workmanship of thy tabrets and of thy pipes was prepared in thee in the day that thou wast created.

timbrel(s)

The timbrel, or tambourine as we know it, has changed probably very little since Biblical times. It is a narrow circular-shelled drum held by the performer's hand and sometimes struck with the other hand or fist. The timbrel might have had a taut head stretched across it, and may have had rattles, or "jingles," inserted in the shell around the drum's circumference. In the 20th Century the tambourine is used in popular as well as in serious music. Before the middle of the 19th Century, the instrument is associated more with folk music, often of the high energy variety. In mediaeval and Renaissance Europe, the instrument was associated more with secular than with sacred music, perhaps almost exclusively. In Biblical references, however, one can interpret rather broad usage of the instrument, associating the timbrel with musical beauty, as well as with its ability to add rhythmic vitality in the dance.

Exodus 15:20 - And Miriam the prophetess, the sister of Aaron, took a timbrel in her hand; and all the women went out after her with timbrels and with dances.

Judges 11:34 - And Jephthah came to Mizpeh unto his house, and, behold, his daughter came out to meet him with timbrels and with dances: and she was his only child; beside her he had neither son nor daughter.

II Samuel 6:5 - And David and all the house of Israel played before the Lord on all manner of instruments made of fir wood, even on harps, and on psalteries, and on timbrels, and on cornets, and on cymbals.

I Chronicles 13:8 - And David and all Israel played before God with all their might, and with singing, and with harps, and with psalteries, and with timbrels, and with cymbals, and with trumpets.

Job 21:12 - They take the timbrel and harp, and rejoice at the sound of the organ.

Psalm 68:25 - The singers went before, the players on instruments followed after; among them were the damsels playing with timbrels.

Psalm 81:2 - Take a psalm, and bring hither the timbrel, the pleasant harp with the psaltery.

Psalm 149:3 - Let them praise his name in the dance: let them sing praises unto him with the <u>timbrel</u> and harp.

Psalm 150:4 - Praise him with the <u>timbrel</u> and dance: praise him with stringed instruments and organs.

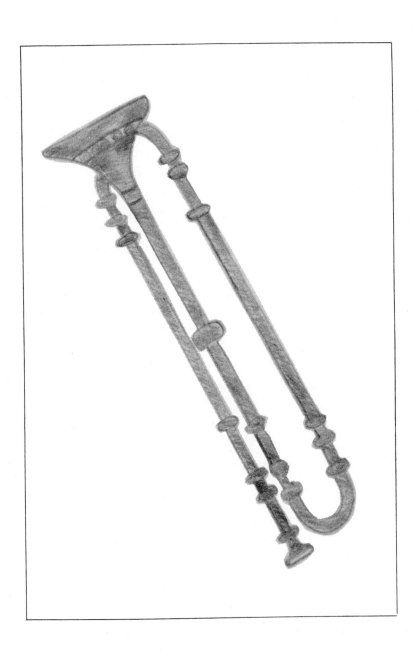

trumpet(s)

The heraldic trumpet has been extant in various forms for many centuries, if not millenia. Its predecessor was the ram's horn, mentioned in this listing, and similar instruments fashioned from the horns of other animals. The trumpet has been used for ages to proclaim forthcoming events in a fanfare manner, as well as to signal troops on the field of battle. The instrument as we know it is a brasswind instrument with a mouthpiece in which the performer's lips buzz to produce the instigating sound. Cylindrical tubing that is bent to take up less space ends in a characteristic "bell" opening that is directed toward the listener. Contemporary trumpets have three "valves" that are depressed by the players' fingers in various combinations to produce a potential chromatic scale in excess of two octaves. The valves are a somewhat recent invention, and most likely would not have been present many centuries ago, resulting in a harmonic rather than a chromatic scale capability being used. In the prior section on the cornet, the difference between the two instruments was discussed and I reiterate my position that early Biblical scholars probably perceived two separate, if similar, instruments here labeled "trumpet" and "cornet," although of course instruments of many centuries ago would be different from those of the present day.

G.F. Handel's oratorio "Messiah," composed in 18th-Century Europe, presents a most appropriate example of art/religious music in the aria titled "The Trumpet Shall Sound," a duet for trumpet and bass voice with orchestral accompaniment. Inspiration for this particular aria with recitative was the New Testament book of First Corinthians, chapter fifteen, verse fifty-two, listed herein, which proclaims:

"for the trumpet shall sound,

and the dead shall be raised incorruptible,

and we shall be changed."

Exodus 19:13 - There shall not an hand touch it, but he shall surely be stoned, or shot through; whether it be beast or man, it shall not live: when the trumpet soundeth long, they shall come up to the mount.

Exodus 19:16 - And it came to pass on the third day in the morning, that there were thunders and lightnings, and a thick cloud upon the mount, and the voice of the trumpet exceeding loud; so that all the people that was in the camp trembled.

Exodus 19:19 - And when the voice of the trumpet sounded long, and waxed louder and louder, Moses spake, and God answered him by a voice.

Exodus 20:18 - And all the people saw the thunderings, and the lightnings, and the noise of the trumpet, and the mountain smoking: and when the people saw it, they removed, and stood afar off.

Leviticus 23:24 - Speak unto the children of Israel, saying, In the seventh month, in the first day of the month, shall ye have a sabbath, a memorial of blowing of trumpets, an holy convocation.

Leviticus 25:9 - Then shalt thou cause the trumpet of the jubile to sound on the tenth day of the seventh month, in the day of atonement shall ye make the trumpet sound throughout all your land.

Numbers 10:2 - Make thee two trumpets of silver; of a whole piece shalt thou make them: that thou mayest use them for the calling of the assembly, and for the journeying of the camps.

Numbers 10:4 - And if they blow but with one trumpet, then the princes, which are heads of the thousands of Israel, shall gather themselves unto thee.

Numbers 10:8 - And sons of Aaron, the priests, shall blow with the trumpets; and they shall be to you for an ordinance for ever throughout your generations.

Numbers 10:9 - And if ye go to war in your land against the enemy that oppresseth you, then ye shall blow an alarm with the trumpets; and ye shall be remembered before the Lord your God, and ye shall be saved from your enemies.

Numbers 10:10 - Also in the day of your gladness, and in your solemn days, and in the beginnings of your months, ye shall blow with the trumpets over your burnt offerings, and over the sacrifices of your peace offerings; that they may be to you for a memorial before your God: I am the Lord your God.

Numbers 29:1 - And in the seventh month, on the first day of the month, ye shall have an holy convocation; ye shall do no servile work: it is a day of blowing the trumpets unto you.

Numbers 31:6 - And Moses sent them to the war, a thousand of every tribe, them and Phinehas the son of Eleazar the priest, to the war, with the holy instruments, and the trumpets to blow in his hand.

Joshua 6:4 - And seven priests shall bear before the ark seven <u>trumpets</u> of rams' horns: and the seventh day ye shall compass the city seven times, and the priests shall blow with the <u>trumpets</u>.

Joshua 6:5 - And it shall come to pass, that when they make a long blast with the ram's horn, and when ye hear the sound of the <u>trumpet,</u>all the people shall shout with a great shout; and the wall of the city shall fall down flat, and the people shall ascend up every man straight before him.

Joshua 6:6 - And Joshua the son of Nun called the priests, and said unto them, Take up the ark of the covenant, and let seven priests bear seven <u>trumpets</u> of rams' horns before the ark of the Lord.

Joshua 6:8 - And it came to pass, when Joshua had spoken unto the people, that the seven priests bearing the seven <u>trumpets</u> of rams' horns passed on before the Lord, and blew with the <u>trumpets</u>: and the ark of the covenant of the Lord followed them.

Joshua 6:9 - And the armed men went before the priests that blew with the <u>trumpets,</u> and the armed men came after the ark, the priests going on, and blowing with the <u>trumpets</u>.

Joshua 6:13 - And seven priests bearing seven <u>trumpets</u> of rams' horns before the ark of the Lord went on continually, and blew with the <u>trumpets</u>: and the armed men went before them; but the rereward came after the ark of the Lord, the priests going on, and blowing with the <u>trumpets</u>.

Joshua 6:16 - And it came to pass at the seventh time, when the priests blew with the <u>trumpets,</u> Joshua said unto the people, Shout; for the Lord hath given you the city.

Joshua 6:20 - So the people shouted when the priests blew with the <u>trumpets</u>: and it came to pass, when the people heard the sound of the <u>trumpet,</u> and the people shouted with a great shout, that the wall fell down flat, so that the people went up into the city, every man straight before him, and they took the city.

Judges 3:27 - And it came to pass, when he was come, that he blew a <u>trumpet</u> in the mountain of Ephraim, and the children of Israel went down with him from the mount, and he before them.

Judges 6:34 - But the Spirit of the Lord came upon Gideon, and he blew a <u>trumpet</u>; and Abi-ezer was gathered after him.

Judges 7:8 - So the people took victuals in their hand, and their <u>trumpets</u>: and he sent all the rest of Israel every man unto his tent, and retained those three hundred men: and the host of Midian was beneath him in the valley.

Judges 7:16 - And he divided the three hundred men into three companies, and he put a <u>trumpet</u> in every man's hand, with empty pitchers, and lamps within the pitchers.

Judges 7:18 - When I blow with a <u>trumpet</u>, I and all that are with me, then blow ye the <u>trumpets</u> also on every side of all the camp, and say, The sword of the Lord, and of Gideon.

Judges 7:19 - So Gideon, and the hundred men that were with him, came unto the outside of the camp in the beginning of the middle watch; and they had but newly set the watch: and they blew the <u>trumpets</u>, and brake the pitchers that were in their hands.

Judges 7:20 - And the three companies blew the <u>trumpets</u>, and brake the pitchers, and held the lamps in their left hands, and the <u>trumpets</u> in their right hands to blow withal: and they cried, The sword of the Lord, and of Gideon.

Judges 7:22 - And the three hundred blew the <u>trumpets</u>, and the Lord set every man's sword against his fellow, even throughout all the host: and the host fled to Beth-shittah in Zererath, and to the border of Abel-meholah, unto Tabbath.

II Samuel 2:28 - So Joab blew a <u>trumpet</u>, and all the people stood still, and pursued after Israel no more, neither fought they any more.

II Samuel 6:15 - So David and all the house of Israel brought up the ark of the Lord with shouting, and with the sound of the <u>trumpet</u>.

II Samuel 15:10 - But Absalom sent spies throughout all the tribes of Israel, saying, As soon as ye hear the sound of the <u>trumpet</u>, then ye shall say, Absalom reigneth in Hebron.

II Samuel 18:16 - And Joab blew the <u>trumpet</u>, and the people returned from pursuing after Israel: for Joab held back the people.

II Samuel 20:1 - And there happened to be there a man of Belial, whose name was Sheba, the son of Bichri, a Benjamite: and he blew a <u>trumpet</u>, and said, We have no part in David, neither have we inheritance in the son of Jesse: every man to his tents, O Israel.

II Samuel 20:22 - Then the woman sent unto all the people in her wisdom. And they cut off the head of Sheba the son of Bichri, and cast it out to Joab. And he blew a <u>trumpet</u>, and they retired from the city, every man to his tent. And Joab returned to Jerusalem unto the king.

I Kings 1:34 - And let Zadok the priest and Nathan the prophet anoint him there king over Israel: and blow ye with the <u>trumpet</u>, and say, God save king Solomon.

I Kings 1:39 - And Zadok the priest took an horn of oil out of the tabernacle, and anointed Solomon. And they blew the <u>trumpet</u>; and all the people said, God save king Solomon.

I Kings 1:41 - And Adonijah and all the guests that were with him heard it as they had made an end of eating. And when Joab heard the sound of the trumpet, he said, Wherefore is this noise of the city being in an uproar?

II Kings 9:13 - Then they hasted, and took every man his garment, and put it under him on the top of the stairs, and blew with trumpets, saying, Jehu is king.

II Kings 11:14 - And when she looked, behold, the king stood by a pillar, as the manner was, and the princes and the trumpeters by the king, and all the people of the land rejoiced, and blew with trumpets: and Athaliah rent her clothes, and cried, Treason, Treason.

II Kings 12:13 - Howbeit there were not made for the house of the Lord bowls of silver, snuffers, basons, trumpets, any vessels of gold, or vessels of silver, of the money that was brought into the house of the Lord:

I Chronicles 13:8 - And David and all Israel played before God with all their might, and with singing, and with harps, and with psalteries, and with timbrels, and with cymbals, and with trumpets.

I Chronicles 15:24 - And Shebaniah, and Jehoshaphat, and Nethaneel, and Amasai, and Zechariah, and Benaiah, and Eliezer, the priests, did blow with the trumpets before the ark of God: and Obed-edom and Jehiah were doorkeepers for the ark.

I Chronicles 15:28 - Thus all Israel brought up the ark of the covenant of the Lord with shouting, and with sound of the cornet, and with trumpets, and with cymbals, making a noise with psalteries and harps.

I Chronicles 16:6 - Benaiah also and Jehaziel the priests with trumpets continually before the ark of the covenant of God.

I Chronicles 16:42 - And with them Heman and Jeduthun with trumpets and cymbals for those that should make a sound, and with musical instruments of God. And the sons of Jeduthun were porters.

II Chronicles 5:12 - Also the Levites which were the singers, all of them Asaph, of Heman, of Jeduthun, with their sons and their brethren, being arrayed in white linen, having cymbals and psalteries and harps, stood at the east end of the altar, and with them an hundred and twenty priests sounding with trumpets:)

II Chronicles 5:13 - It came even to pass, as the trumpeters and singers were as one, to make one sound to be heard in praising and thanking the Lord; and when they lifted up their voice with the trumpets and cymbals and instruments of musick, and praised the Lord, saying, For he is good; for his mercy endureth for ever: that then the house was filled with a cloud, even the house of the Lord;

II Chronicles 7:6 - And the priests waited on their offices: the Levites also with instruments of musick of the Lord, which David the king had made to praise the Lord, because his mercy endureth for ever, when David praised by their ministry; and the priests sounded <u>trumpets</u> before them, and all Israel stood.

II Chronicles 13:12 - And, behold, God himself is with us for our captain, and his priests with sounding <u>trumpets</u> to cry alarm against you. O children of Israel, fight ye not against the Lord God of your fathers; for ye shall not prosper.

II Chronicles 13:14 - And when Judah looked back, behold, the battle was before and behind: and they cried unto the Lord, and the priests sounded with the <u>trumpets</u>.

II Chronicles 15:14 - And they sware unto the Lord with a loud voice, and with shouting, and with <u>trumpets,</u> and with cornets.

II Chronicles 20:28 - And they came to Jerusalem with psalteries and harps and <u>trumpets</u> unto the house of the Lord.

II Chronicles 23:13 - And she looked, and, behold, the king stood at his pillar at the entering in, and the princes and the <u>trumpets</u> by the king; and all the people of the land rejoiced, and sounded with <u>trumpets,</u> also the singers with instruments of musick, and such as taught to sing praise. Then Athaliah rent her clothes, and said, Treason, Treason.

II Chronicles 29:26 - And the Levites stood with the instruments of David, and the priests with the <u>trumpets.</u>

II Chronicles 29:27 - And Hezekiah commanded to offer the burnt offering upon the altar. And when the burnt offering began, the song of the Lord began also with the <u>trumpets,</u> and with the instruments ordained by David king of Israel.

Ezra 3:10 - And when the builders laid the foundation of the temple of the Lord, they set the priests in their apparel with <u>trumpets,</u> and the Levites the sons of Asaph with cymbals, to praise the Lord, after the ordinance of David king of Israel.

Nehemiah 4:18 - For the builders, every one had his sword girded by his side, and so builded. And he that sounded the <u>trumpet</u> was by me.

Nehemiah 4:20 - In what place therefore ye hear the sound of the <u>trumpet</u>, resort ye thither unto us: our God shall fight for us.

Nehemiah 12:35 - And certain of the priests' sons with <u>trumpets</u>; namely, Zechariah the son of Jonathan, the son of Shemaiah, the son of Mattaniah, the son of Michaiah, the son of Zaccur, the son of Asaph:

Nehemiah 12:41 - And the priests; Eliakim, Maaseiah, Miniamin, Michaiah, Elioenai, Zechariah, and Hananiah, with trumpets;

Job 39:24 - He swalloweth the ground with fierceness and rage: neither believeth he that it is the sound of the trumpet.

Job 39:25 - He saith among the trumpets, Ha, ha; and he smelleth the battle afar off, the thunder of the captains, and the shouting.

Psalm 47:5 - God is gone up with a shout, the Lord with the sound of a trumpet.

Psalm 81:3 - Blow up the trumpet in the new moon, in the time appointed, on our solemn feast day.

Psalm 98:6 - With trumpets and sound of cornet make a joyful noise before the Lord, the King.

Psalm 150:3 - Praise him with the sound of the trumpet: praise him with the psaltery and harp.

Isaiah 18:3 - All ye inhabitants of the world, and dwellers on the earth, see ye, when he lifteth up an ensign on the mountains; and when he bloweth a trumpet, hear ye.

Isaiah 27:13 - And it shall come to pass in that day, that the great trumpet shall be blown, and they shall come which were ready to perish in the land of Assyria, and the outcasts in the land of Egypt, and shall worship the Lord in the holy mount at Jerusalem.

Isaiah 58:1 - Cry aloud, spare not, lift up thy voice like a trumpet, and shew my people their transgression, and the house of Jacob their sins.

Jeremiah 4:5 - Declare ye in Judah, and publish in Jerusalem; and say, Blow ye the trumpet in the land: cry, gather together, and say, Assemble yourselves, and let us go into the defenced cities.

Jeremiah 4:19 - My bowels, my bowels! I am pained at my very heart; my heart maketh a noise in me; I cannot hold my peace, because thou hast heard, O my soul, the sound of the trumpet, the alarm of war.

Jeremiah 4:21 - How long shall I see the standard, and hear the sound of the trumpet?

Jeremiah 6:1 - O ye children of Benjamin, gather yourselves to flee out of the midst of Jerusalem, and blow the trumpet in Tekoa, and set up a sign of fire in Beth-haccerem: for evil appeareth out of the north, and great destruction.

Jeremiah 6:17 - Also I set watchmen over you, saying, Hearken to the sound of the trumpet. But they said, We will not hearken.

Jeremiah 42:14 - Saying, No; but we will go into the land of Egypt, where we shall see no war, nor hear the sound of the trumpet, nor have hunger of bread; and there will we dwell:

Jeremiah 51:27 - Set ye up a standard in the land, blow the trumpet among the nations, prepare the nations against her, call together against her the kingdoms of Ararat, Minni, and Ashchenaz; appoint a captain against her; cause the horses to come up as rough caterpillers.

Ezekiel 7:14 - They have blown the trumpet, even to make all ready; but none goeth to the battle: for my wrath is upon all the multitude thereof.

Ezekiel 33:3 - If when he seeth the sword come upon the land, he blow the trumpet, and warn the people;

Ezekiel 33:4 - Then whosoever heareth the sound of the trumpet, and taketh not warning; if the sword come, and take him away, his blood shall be upon his own head.

Ezekiel 33:5 - He heard the sound of the trumpet, and took not warning; his blood shall be upon him. But he that taketh warning shall deliver his soul.

Ezekiel 33:6 - But if the watchman see the sword come, and blow not the trumpet, and the people be not warned; if the sword come, and take any person from among them, he is taken away in his iniquity; but his blood will I require at the watchman's hand.

Hosea 5:8 - Blow ye the cornet in Gibeah, and the trumpet in Ramah: cry aloud at Beth-aven, after thee, O Benjamin.

Hosea 8:1 - Set the trumpet to thy mouth. He shall come as an eagle against the house of the Lord, because they have transgressed my covenant, and trespassed against my law.

Joel 2:1 - Blow ye the trumpet in Zion, and sound an alarm in my holy mountain: let all the inhabitants of the land tremble: for the day of the Lord cometh, for it is nigh at hand;

Joel 2:15 - Blow the trumpet in Zion, sanctify a fast, call a solemn assembly:

Amos 2:2 - But I will send a fire upon Moab, and it shall devour the palaces of Kirioth: and Moab shall die with tumult, with shouting, and with the sound of the trumpet:

Amos 3:6 - Shall a trumpet be blown in the city, and the people not be afraid:? shall there be evil in a city, and the Lord hath not done it?

Zephaniah 1:16 - A day of the trumpet and alarm against the fenced cities, and against the high towers.

Zechariah 9:14 - And the Lord shall be seen over them, and his arrow shall go forth as the lightning: and the Lord God shall blow the <u>trumpet,</u> and shall go with whirlwinds of the south.

Matthew 6:2 - Therefore when thou doest thine alms, do not sound a <u>trumpet</u> before thee, as the hypocrites do in the synagogues and in the streets, that they may have glory of men. Verily I say unto you, They have their reward.

Matthew 24:31 - And he shall send his angels with a great sound of a <u>trumpet,</u> and they shall gather together his elect from the four winds, from one end of heaven to the other.

I Corinthians 14:8 - For if the <u>trumpet</u> give an uncertain sound, who shall prepare himself to the battle?

I Corinthians 15:52 - In a moment, in the twinkling of an eye, at the last trump: for the <u>trumpet</u> shall sound, and the dead shall be raised incorruptible, and we shall be changed.

Hebrews 12:19 - And the sound of a <u>trumpet,</u> and the voice of words; which voice they that heard intreated that the word should not be spoken to them any more:

Revelation 1:10 - I was in the Spirit on the Lord's day, and heard behind me a great voice, as of a <u>trumpet,</u>

Revelation 4:1 - After this I looked, and, behold, a door was opened in heaven: and the first voice which I heard was as it were of a <u>trumpet</u> talking with me; which said, Come up hither, and I will shew thee things which must be hereafter.

Revelation 8:2 - And I saw the seven angels which stood before God; and to them were given seven <u>trumpets.</u>

Revelation 8:6 - And the seven angels which had the seven <u>trumpets</u> prepared themselves to sound.

Revelation 8:13 - And I beheld, and heard an angel flying through the midst of heaven, saying with a loud voice, Woe, woe, woe, to the inhabiters of the earth by reason of the other voices of the <u>trumpet</u> of the three angels, which are yet to sound!

Revelation 9:14 - Saying to the sixth angel which had the <u>trumpet,</u> Loose the four angels which are bound in the great river Euphrates.

<u>trumpeters</u>

II Kings 11:14 - And when she looked, behold, the king stood by a pillar, as the manner was, and the princes and the <u>trumpeters</u> by the king, and all the people of the land rejoiced, and blew with trumpets: and Athaliah rent her clothes, and cried, Treason, Treason.

II Chronicles 5:13 - It came even to pass, as the <u>trumpeters</u> and singers were as one, to make one sound to be heard in praising and thanking the Lord; and when they lifted up their voice with the trumpets and cymbals and instruments of musick, and praised the Lord, saying, For he is good; for his mercy endureth for ever: that then the house was filled with a cloud, even the house of the Lord;

II Chronicles 29:28 - And all the congregation worshipped, and the singers sang, and the <u>trumpeters</u> sounded: and all this continued until the burnt offering was finished.

Revelation 18:22 - And the voice of harpers, and musicians, and of pipers, and <u>trumpeters,</u> shall be heard no more at all in thee; and no craftsman, of whatsoever craft he be, shall be found any more in thee; and the sound of a millstone shall be heard no more at all in thee;

viol(s)

The soft, gentle sounding viol is a type of bowed stringed instrument, best known to music historians as the precursor to the violin family of instruments, and popular in Europe in the 16th and 17th Centuries. Its four locations in the Bible seem to summarize the basic ideas regarding music and musical instruments throughout the holy Scriptures. The viol is mentioned by itself in the book of Isaiah and with other instruments earlier in that same book. The viol is associated with musical beauty in the fifth chapter of Amos, and with noise in the fourteenth chapter of Isaiah. The instrument is likewise mentioned with Scripturally approved human behavior, as in the sixth chapter of Amos, as well as with disapproved human behavior, as in the fifth chapter of Isaiah. Thus the viol can serve as typical of Biblical instruments: quite real in an aesthetic sense, yet capable of being used with good or evil by women and men.

Isaiah 5:12 - And the harp, and the viol, the tabret, and pipe, and wine, are in their feasts: but they regard not the work of the Lord, neither consider the operation of his hands.

Isaiah 14:11 - Thy pomp is brought down to the grave, and the noise of thy viols: the worm is spread under thee, and the worms cover thee.

Amos 5:23 - Take thou away from me the noise of thy songs; for I will not hear the melody of thy viols.

Amos 6:5 - That chant to the sound of the viol, and invent to themselves instruments of musick, like David;

Section II: Song Texts in the Bible

Foreword to Section II

In contrast to Section I of this monograph, Section II, entitled Song Texts in the Bible, has a minimum of editorial commentary and a maximum of Scriptural text. The section is in three subsections, including an essay on the definition of song, a collection of several individual song texts from various parts of the Bible, and the entire Song of Solomon. The latter of course is quite lengthy, and certainly a valuable portion of Scriptural song literature. This section generally contains a considerable variety of literature, spanning from the non-religious to the extremely devotional. These readings are more complete in thought than the extractions that make up Section I, and summarily show a wide range of ideas and degree of devotion in the various passages. What is perhaps most notable to the reader who habitually concentrates on the New Testament of the Bible, is that many of the Old Testament readings are indeed reflective--not only precursors--of New Testament literature and ideology.

Essay: On the Definition of Song

At times only the philosophically minded would be interested in defining the word "song." However, consideration of such mental exercise is at the heart of the matter of delineating "songs" in the Bible. Generally, a song would be text, or words, set to music, especially to a melody. Of course the holy Scriptures do not contain notated music, and of course we do not have audio recordings of music performed many centuries ago.

Further, some observers would define a song text as being poetic in nature, rather than prose; in other words, it should contain certain elements of rhythm and meter, and perhaps rhyme. Obviously several translations into numerous languages over a period of time would cause the original song text to most likely lose much of its rhythm, meter, and perhaps rhyme, since each language is different from every other language in pronunciation and syntax, among other aspects. Likewise, exact meanings often do not transfer precisely from one language to another.

A starting point to finding song texts in the Bible is to research various appearances of the word "song" and to include those passages that are described directly as songs. Syntax, poetic elements, and lyrical aspects sometimes can give a hint as to which passages were probably song texts, but likewise many have probably been changed over the centuries.

Thus the following listing is imperfect at worst, and elucidative at best. Some observers would argue that a given Biblical edition might be more true to the original Hebrew or Greek "poetry" than another edition, but for the purposes of inclusion in this collection, the editor has chosen to include probable song texts, realizing that the listing is most likely imperfect. The word "text" has been used, rather than the contemporary word "lyric," with the understanding that the song texts are more literal than musical in this rendition and at this point in time. However, one good result of such a collection as this might someday be the motivation for a composer to create original music for the texts herein, since they are conveniently grouped together. Contemporary musical composition does allow for variety in verbal rhythm, meter, and rhyme elements, as well as the inclusion of dramatic reading in addition to melodic rendition of text. Of course some traditional types of vocal music such as opera and oratorio often involve both declamatory and lyrical expression, usually called recitative and aria.

In conclusion, this author/editor defines "song" rather broadly, as the word is used in the Bible. A possible definition thus could involve "lyrical production in a verbal and melodic manner that originates in the soul of a human being," to incorporate a religious orientation. The melodic aspect of Biblical songs is lost in its original forms, but certainly can be created in contemporary contexts.

Song of Moses

Exodus 15:1 - Then sang Moses and the children of Israel this song unto the Lord, and spake, saying, I will sing unto the Lord, for he hath triumphed gloriously: the horse and his rider hath he thrown into the sea.

2   The Lord is my strength and song, and he is become my salvation: he is my God, and I will prepare him an habitation; my father's God, and I will exalt him.

3   The Lord is a man of war: the Lord is his name.

4   Pharaoh's chariots and his host hath he cast into the sea: his chosen captains also are drowned in the Red sea.

5   The depths have covered them: they sank into the bottom as a stone.

6   Thy right hand, O Lord, is become glorious in power; thy right hand, O Lord, hath dashed in pieces the enemy.

7   And in the greatness of thine excellency thou hast overthrown them that rose up against thee: thou sentest forth thy wrath, which consumed them as stubble.

8   And with the blast of thy nostrils the waters were gathered together, the floods stood upright as an heap, and the depths were congealed in the heart of the sea.

9   The enemy said, I will pursue, I will overtake, I will divide the spoil; my lust shall be satisfied upon them; I will draw my sword, my hand shall destroy them.

10   Thou didst blow with thy wind, the sea covered them: they sank, as lead in the mighty waters.

11   Who is like unto thee, O Lord, among the gods? Who is like thee, glorious in holiness, fearful in praises, doing wonders?

12   Thou stretchedst out thy right hand, the earth swallowed them.

13   Thou in thy mercy hast led forth the people which thou hast redeemed: thou hast guided them in thy strength unto thy holy habitation.

14   The people shall hear, and be afraid: sorrow shall take hold on the inhabitants of Palestine.

15   Then the dukes of Edom shall be amazed; the mighty men of Moab, trembling shall take hold upon them; all the inhabitants of Canaan shall melt away.

16   Fear and dread shall fall upon them; by the greatness of thine arm they shall be as still as a stone; till thy people pass over, O Lord, till the people pass over, which thou hast purchased.

17   Thou shalt bring them in, and plant them in the mountain of thine inheritance, in the place, O Lord, which thou hast made for thee to swell in, in the Sanctuary, O Lord, which thy hands have established.

18   The Lord shall reign for ever and ever.

Song of Miriam

Exodus 15:21 - And Miriam answered them, Sing ye to the Lord, for he hath triumphed gloriously; the horse and his rider hath he thrown into the sea.

Three Poetic Fragments

From the Book of Numbers

Numbers 21:14 - Wherefore it is said in the book of the wars of the Lord, What he did in the Red sea, and in the brooks of Arnon,

15   And at the stream of the brooks that goeth down to the dwelling of Ar, and lieth upon the border of Moab.

Song of the Well

Numbers 21:16 - And from thence they went to Beer: that is the well whereof the Lord spake unto Moses, Gather the people together, and I will give them water.

17   Then Israel sang this song, Spring up, O well; sing ye unto it:

18   The princes digged the well, the nobles of the people digged it, by the direction of the lawgiver, with their staves. And from the wilderness they went to Mattanah:

Taunt Song

Numbers 21:28 For there is a fire gone out of Heshbon, a flame from the city of Sihon: it hath consumed Ar of Moab, and the lords of the high places of Arnon.

29   Woe to thee, Moab! thou art undone, O people of Chemosh: he hath given his sons that escaped, and his daughters, into captivity unto Sihon king of the Amorites.

30   We have shot at them; Heshbon is perished even unto Dibon, and we have laid them waste even unto Nophah, which reacheth unto Medeba.

Song, or Psalm, of Moses

Deuteronomy 32:1 - Give ear, O ye heavens, and I will speak; and hear, O earth, the words of my mouth.

2   My doctrine shall drop as the rain, my speech shall distil as the dew, as the small rain upon the tender herb, and as the showers upon the grass:

3   Because I will publish the name of the Lord: ascribe ye greatness unto our God.

4   He is the Rock, his work, is perfect: for all his ways are judgment: a God of truth and without iniquity, just and right is he.

5   They have corrupted themselves, their spot is not the spot of his children: they are a peverse and crooked generation.

6   Do ye thus requite the Lord, O foolish people and unwise? is not he thy father that hath bought thee? hath he not made thee, and established thee?

7   Remember the days of old, consider the years of many generations: ask thy father, and he will shew thee; thy elders, and they will tell thee.

8   When the most High divided to the nations their inheritance, when he separated the sons of Adam, he set the bounds of the people according to the number of the children of Israel.

9   For the Lord's portion is his people; Jacob is the lot of his inheritance.

10   He found him in a desert land, and in the waste howling wilderness; he led him about, he instructed him, he kept him as the apple of his eye.

11   As an eagle stirreth up her nest, fluttereth over her young, spreadeth abroad her wings, taketh them, beareth them on her wings:

12   So the Lord alone did lead him, and there was no strange god with him.

13   He made him ride on the high places of the earth, that he might eat the increase of the fields; and he made him to suck honey out of the rock, and oil out of the flinty rock;

14   Butter of kine, and milk of sheep, with fat of lambs, and rams of the breed of Bashan, and goats, with the fat of kidneys of wheat; and thou didst drink the pure blood of the grape.

15   But Jeshurun waxed fat, and kicked: thou art waxen fat, thou art grown thick, thou art covered with fatness; then he forsook God which made him, and lightly esteemed the Rock of his salvation.

16   They provoked him to jealousy with strange gods, with abominations provoked they him to anger.

17   They sacrificed unto devils, not to God; to gods whom they knew not, to new gods that came newly up, whom your fathers feared not.

18   Of the Rock that begat thee thou art unmindful, and hast forgotten God that formed thee.

19   And when the Lord saw it, he abhorred them, because of the provoking of his sons, and of his daughters.

20   And he said, I will hide my face from them, I will see what their end shall be: for they are a very forward generation, children in whom is no faith.

21   They have moved me to jealousy with that which is not God; they have provoked me to anger with their vanities: and I will move them to jealousy with those which are not a people; I will provoke them to anger with a foolish nation.

22   For a fire is kindled in mine anger, and shall burn unto the lowest hell, and shall consume the earth with her increase, and set on fire the foundations of the mountains.

23   I will heap mischiefs upon them; I will spend mine arrows upon them.

24   They shall be burnt with hunger, and devoured with burning heat, and with bitter destruction: I will also send the teeth of beasts upon them, with the poison of serpents of the dust.

25   The sword without, and terror within, shall destroy both the young man and the virgin, the suckling also with the man of gray hairs.

26   I said, I would scatter them into corners, I would make the remembrance of them to cease from among men:

27   Were it not that I feared the wrath of the enemy, lest their adversaries should behave themselves strangely, and lest they should say, Our hand is high, and the Lord hath not done all this.

28   For they are a nation void of counsel, neither is there any understanding in them.

29   O that they were wise, that they understood this, that they would consider their latter end!

30   How should one chase a thousand, and two put ten thousand to flight, except their Rock had sold them, and the Lord had shut them up?

31   For their rock is not as our Rock, even our enemies themselves being judges.

32   For their vine is of the vine of Sodom, and of the fields of Gomorrah: their grapes are grapes of gall, their clusters are bitter:

33   Their wine is the poison of dragons, and the cruel venom of asps.

34   Is not this laid up in store with me, and sealed up among my treasures?

35   To me belongeth vengeance, and recompense; their foot shall slide in due time: for the day of their calamity is at hand, and the things that shall come upon them make haste.

36   For the Lord shall judge his people, and repent himself for his servants, when he seeth that their power is gone, and there is none shut up, or left.

37   And he shall say, Where are their gods, their rock in whom they trusted,

38   Which did eat the fat of their sacrifices, and drank the wine of their drink offerings? let them rise up and help you, and be your protection.

39   See now that I, even I, am he, and there is no god with me: I kill, and I make alive; I wound, and I heal: neither is there any that can deliver out of my hand.

40   For I lift up my hand to heaven, and say, I live for ever.

41   If I whet my glittering sword, and mime hand take hold on judgment; I will render vengeance to mind enemies, and will reward them that hate me.

42   I will make mine arrows drunk with blood, and my sword shall devout flesh; and that with the blood of the slain and of the captives, from the beginning of revenges upon the enemy.

43   Rejoice, O ye nations, with his people: for he will avenge the blood of his servants, and will render vengeance to his adversaries, and will be merciful unto his land, and to his people.

44   And Moses came and spake all the words of this song in the ears of the people, he, and Hoshea the son of Nun.

45   And Moses made an end of speaking all these words to all Israel:

120

46   And he said unto them, Set your hearts unto all the words which I testify among you this day, which ye shall command your children to observe to do, all the words of this law.

47   For it is not a vain thing for you; because it is your life: and through this thing ye shall prolong your days in the land, whither ye go over Jordan to possess it.

48   And the Lord spake unto Moses that selfsame day, saying,

49   Get thee up into this mountain Abarim, unto mount Nebo, which is in the land of Moab, that is over against Jericho; and behold the land of Canaan, which I give unto the children of Israel for a possession:

50   And die in the mount whither thou goest up, and be gathered unto thy people; as Aaron thy brother died in mount Hor, and was gathered unto his people:

51   Because ye trespassed against me among the children of Israel at the waters of Meribah-Kadesh, in the wilderness of Zin; because ye sanctified me not in the midst of the children of Israel.

52   Yet thou shalt see the land before thee; but thou shalt not go thither unto the land which I give the children of Israel.

Song of Deborah

Judges 5:1 - Then sang Deborah and Barak the son of Abinoam on that day, saying,

2   Praise ye the Lord for the avenging of Israel, when the people willingly offered themselves.

3   Hear, O ye kings; give ear, O ye princes; I, even I, will sing unto the Lord; I will sing praise to the Lord God of Israel.

4   Lord, when thou wentest out of Seir, when thou marchedst out of the field of Edom, the earth trembled, and the heavens dropped, the clouds also dropped water.

5   The mountains melted from before the Lord, even that Sinai from before the Lord God of Israel.

6   In the days of Shamgar the son of Anath, in the days of Jael, the highways were unoccupied, and the travellers walked through byways.

7   The inhabitants of the villages ceased, they ceased in Israel, until that I Deborah arose, that I arose a mother in Israel.

8   They chose new gods; then was war in the gates: was there a shield or spear seen among forty thousand in Israel?

9   My heart is toward the governors of Israel, that offered themselves willingly among the people. Bless ye the Lord.

10   Speak, ye that ride on white asses, ye that sit in judgment, and walk by the way.

11   They that are delivered from the noise of archers in the places of drawing water, there shall they rehearse the righteous acts of the Lord, even the righteous acts toward the inhabitants of his villages in Israel: then shall the people of the Lord go down to the gates.

12   Awake, awake, Deborah: awake, awake, utter a song: arise, Barak, and lead thy captivity captive, thou son of Abinoam.

13   Then he made him that remaineth have dominion over the nobles among the people: the Lord made me have dominion over the mighty.

14   Out of Ephraim was there a root of them against Amalek; after thee, Benjamin, among thy people; out of Machir came down governors, and out of Zebulun they that handle the pen of the writer.

15   And the princes of Issachar were with Deborah; even Issachar, and also Barak: he has sent on foot into the valley. For the divisions of Reuben there were great thoughts of heart.

16   Why abodest thou among the sheepfolds, to hear the bleatings of the flocks? For the divisions of Reuben there were great searchings of heart.

17   Gilead abode beyond Jordan: and why did Dan remain in ships? Asher continued on the sea shore, and abode in his breaches.

18   Zebulun and Naphtali were a people that jeoparded their lives unto the death in the high places of the field.

19   The kings came and fought, then fought the kings of Canaan in Taanach by the waters of Megiddo; they took no gain of money.

20   They fought from heaven; the stars in their courses fought against Sisera.

21   The river of Kishon swept them away, that ancient river, the river Kishon. O my soul, thou hast trodden down strength.

22   Then were the horsehoofs broken by the means of the pransings, the pransings of their mighty ones.

23   Curse ye Meroz, said the angel of the Lord, curse ye bitterly the inhabitants thereof; because they came not to the help of the Lord, to the help of the Lord against the mighty.

24   Blessed above women shall Jael the wife of Heber the Kenite be, blessed shall she be above women in the tent.

25   He asked water, and she gave him milk; she brought forth butter in a lordly dish.

26   She put her hand to the nail, and her right hand to the workmen's hammer; and with the hammer she smote Sisera, she smote off his head, when she had pierced and stricken through his temples.

27   At her feet he bowed, he fell, he lay down: at her feet he bowed, he fell: where he bowed, there he fell down dead.

28   The mother of Sisera looked out at a window, and cried through the lattice, Why is his chariot so long in coming? why tarry the wheels of his chariots?

29   Her wise ladies answered yea, yea, she returned answer to herself,

30   Have they not sped? have they not divided the prey; to every man a damsel or two; to Sisera a prey of divers colours of needlework on both sides, meet for the necks of them that take the spoil?

31   So let all thine enemies perish, O Lord: but let them that love him be as the sun when he goeth forth in his might. And the land had rest forty years.

Song of Hannah

I Samuel 2:1 - And Hannah prayed, and said, My heart rejoiceth in the Lord, mine horn is exalted in the Lord: my mouth is enlarged over mine enemies; because I rejoice in thy salvation.

2   There is none holy as the Lord: for there is none beside thee: neither is there any rock like our God.

3   Talk no more so exceeding proudly; let not arrogancy come out of your mouth: for the Lord is a God of knowledge, and by him actions are weighed.

4   The bows of the mighty men are broken, and they that stumbled are girded with strength.

5   They that were full have hired out themselves for bread; and they that were hungry ceased: so that the barren hath born seven; and she that hath many children is waxed feeble.

6   The Lord killeth, and maketh alive: he bringeth down to the grave, and bringeth up.

7   The Lord maketh poor, and maketh rich: he bringeth low, and lifteth up.

8   He raiseth up the poor out of the dust, and lifteth up the beggar from the dunghill, to set them among princes, and to make them inherit the throne of glory: for the pillars of the earth are the Lord's, and he hath set the world upon them.

9   He will keep the feet of his saints, and the wicked shall be silent in darkness; for by strength shall no man prevail.

10   The adversaries of the Lord shall be broken to pieces; out of heaven shall he thunder upon them: the Lord shall judge the ends of the earth; and he shall give strength unto his king, and exalt the horn of his anointed.

Elegy for Saul and Jonathan

II Samuel 1:17 - And David lamented with his lamentation over Saul and over Jonathan his son:

18   (Also he bade them teach the children of Judah the use of the bow: behold, it is written in the book of Jasher.)

19   The beauty of Israel is slain upon thy high places: how are the mighty fallen!

20   Tell it not in Gath, publish it not in the streets of Askelon; lest the daughters of the Philistines rejoice, lest the daughters of the uncircumcised triumph.

21   Ye mountains of Gilboa, let there be no dew, neither let there be rain, upon you, nor fields of offerings: for there the shield of the mighty is vilely cast away, the shield of Saul, as though he had not been anointed with oil.

22   From the blood of the slain, from the fat of the mighty, the bow of Jonathan turned not back, and the sword of Saul returned not empty.

23   Saul and Jonathan were lovely and pleasant in their lives, and in their death they were not divided: they were swifter than eagles, they were stronger than lions.

24   Ye daughters of Israel, weep over Saul, who clothed you in scarlet, with other delights, who put on ornaments of gold upon your apparel.

25   How are the mighty fallen in the midst of the battle! O Jonathan, thou wast slain in thine high places.

26   I am distressed for thee, my brother Jonathan: very pleasant hast thou been unto me: thy love to me was wonderful, passing the love of women.

27   How are the mighty fallen, and the weapons of war perished!

Hymn of Praise

II Samuel 22:1 - And David spake unto the Lord the words of this song in the day that the Lord had delivered him out of the hand of all his enemies, and out of the hand of Saul:

2   And he said, The Lord is my rock, and my fortress, and my deliverer;

3   The God of my rock; in him will I trust: he is my shield, and the horn of my salvation, my high tower, and my refuge, my saviour; thou savest me from violence.

4   I will call on the Lord, who is worthy to be praised: so shall I be saved from mine enemies.

5   When the waves of death compassed me, the floods of ungodly men made me afraid;

6   The sorrows of hell compassed me about; the snares of death prevented me;

7   In my distress I called upon the Lord, and cried to my God: and he did hear my voice out of his temple, and my cry did enter into his ears.

8   Then the earth shook and trembled; the foundations of heaven moved and shook, because he was wroth.

9   There went up a smoke out of his nostrils, and fire out of his mouth devoured: coals were kindled by it.

10   He bowed the heavens also, and came down; and darkness was under his feet.

11   And he rode upon a cherub, and did fly: and he was seen upon the wings of the wind.

12   And he made darkness pavilions round about him, dark waters, and thick clouds of the skies.

13   Through the brightness before him were coals of fire kindled.

14   The Lord thundered from heaven, and the most High uttered his voice.

15   And he sent out arrows, and scattered them; lightning, and discomfited them.

16   And the channels of the sea appeared, the foundations of the world were discovered, at the rebuking of the Lord, at the blast of the breath of his nostrils.

17   He sent from above, he took me; he drew me out of many waters;

18   He delivered me from my strong enemy,and from them that hated me: for they were too strong for me.

19   They prevented me in the day of my calamity: but the Lord was my stay.

20   He brought me forth also into a large place: he delivered me, because he delighted in me.

21   The Lord rewarded me according to my righteousness: according to the cleanness of my hands hath he recompensed me.

22   For I have kept the ways of the Lord, and have not wickedly departed from my God.

23   For all his judgments were before me: and as for his statutes, I did not depart from them.

24   I was also upright before him, and have kept myself from mine iniquity.

25   Therefore the Lord hath recompensed me according to my righteousness; according to my cleanness in his eye sight.

26   With the merciful thou wilt shew thyself merciful, and with the upright man thou wilt shew thyself upright.

27   With the purse thou wilt shew thyself pure; and with the froward thou wilt shew thyself unsavoury.

28   And the afflicted people thou wilt save: but thine eyes are upon the haughty, that thou mayest bring them down.

29   For thou art my lamp,m O Lord: and the Lord will I lighten my darkness.

30   For by thee I have run through a troop: by my God have I leaped over a wall.

31   As for God, his way is perfect; the word of the Lord is tried: he is a buckler to all them that trust in him.

32   For who is God, save the Lord? and who is a rock, save our God?

33   God is my strength and power: and he maketh my way perfect.

34   He maketh my feet like hinds' feet: and setteth me upon my high places.

35   He teacheth my hands to war: so that a bow of steel is broken by mine arms.

36   Thou hast also given me the shield of thy salvation: and thy gentleness hath made me great.

37   Thou hast enlarged my steps under me; so that my feet did not slip.

38   I have pursued mine enemies, and destroyed them; and turned not again until I had consumed them.

39   And I have consumed them, and wounded them, that they could not arise: yea, they are fallen under my feet.

40   For thou hast girded me with strength to battle: them that rose up against me hast thou subdued under me.

41   Thou hast also given me the necks of mine enemies, that I might destroy them that hate me.

42   They looked, but there was none to save; even unto the Lord, but he answered them not.

43   Then did I beat them as small as the dust of the earth, I did stamp them as the mire of the street, and did spread them abroad.

44   Thou also hast delivered me from the strivings of my people, thou hast kept me to be head of the heathen: a people which I knew not shall serve me.

45   Strangers shall submit themselves unto me: as soon as they hear, they shall be obedient unto me.

46   Strangers shall fade away, and they shall be afraid out of their close places.

47   The Lord liveth; and blessed be my rock; and exalted be the God of the rock of my salvation.

48   It is God that avengeth me, and that bringeth down the people under me,

49   And that bringeth me forth from mine enemies: thou also hast lifted me up on high above them that rose up against me: thou hast delivered me from the violent mad.

50   Therefore I will give thanks unto thee, O Lord, among the heathen, and I will sing praises unto thy name.

51   He is the tower of salvation for his king: and sheweth mercy to his anointed, unto David, and to his seed for evermore.

Hymn

II Samuel 23:1 - Now these be the last words of David. David the son of Jesse said, and the man who was raised up on high, the anointed of the God of Jacob, and the sweet psalmist of Israel, said,

2 The Spirit of the Lord spake by me, and his word was in my tongue.

3 The God of Israel said, the rock of Israel spake to me, He that ruleth over men must be just, ruling in the fear of God.

4 And he shall be as the light of the morning, when the sun riseth, even a morning without clouds; as the tender grass springing out of the earth by clear shining after rain.

5 Although my house be not so with God; yet he hath made with me an everlasting covenant, ordered in all things, and sure: for this is all my salvation, and all my desire, although he make it not to grow.

6 But the sons of Belial shall be all of them as thorns thrust away, because they cannot be taken with hands:

7 But the man that shall touch them must be fenced with iron and the staff of a spear; and they shall be utterly burned with fire in the same place.

Song of Victory

Isaiah 26:1 - In that day shall this song be sung in the land of Judah; We have a strong city; salvation will God appoint for walls and bulwarks.

2   Open ye the gates, that the righteous nation which keepeth the truth may enter in.

3   Thou wilt keep him in perfect peace, whose mind is stayed on thee: because he trusteth in thee.

4   Trust ye in the Lord for ever: for in the Lord Jehovah is everlasting strength:

5   For he bringeth down them that dwell on high; the lofty city, he layeth it low; he layeth it low, even to the ground; he bringeth it even to the dust.

6   The foot shall tread it down, even the feet of the poor, and the steps of the needy.

Song of Apocalypse

Isaiah 26:7 - The way of the just is uprightness: thou, most upright, dost weigh the path of the just.

8   Yea, in the way of thy judgments, O Lord, have we waited for thee; the desire of our soul is to thy name, and to the remembrance of thee.

9   With my soul have I desired thee in the night; yea, with my spirit within me will I seek thee early: for when thy judgments are in the earth, the inhabitants of the world will learn righteousness.

10   Let favour be shewed to the wicked, yet will he not learn righteousness: in the land of uprightness will he deal unjustly, and will not behold the majesty of the Lord.

11   Lord, when thy hand is lifted up, they will not see; but they shall see, and be ashamed for their envy at the people; yea, the fire of thine enemies shall devour them.

12   Lord, thou wilt ordain peace for us: for thou also hast wrought all our works in us.

13   O Lord our God, other lords beside thee have had dominion over us: but by thee only will we make mention of thy name.

14   They are dead, they shall not live; they are deceased, they shall not rise: therefore hast thou visited and destroyed them, and made all their memory to perish.

15   Thou hast increased the nation, O Lord, thou hast increased the nation: thou art glorified: thou hadst removed it far unto all the ends of the earth.

16   Lord, in trouble have they visited thee, they poured out a prayer when thy chastening was upon them.

17   Like as a woman with child, that draweth near the time of her delivery, is in pain, and crieth out in her pangs; so have we been in thy sight, O Lord.

18   We have been with child, we have been in pain, we have as it were brought forth wind; we have not wrought any deliverance in the earth; neither have the inhabitants of the world fallen.

19   Thy dead men shall live, together with my dead body shall they arise. Awake and sing, ye that dwell in dust: for thy dew is as the dew of herbs, and the earth shall cast out the dead.

Song of Thanksgiving

Isaiah 38:9 - The writing of Hezekiah king of Judah, when he had been sick, and was recovered of his sickness:

10   I said in the cutting off of my days, I shall go to the gates of the grave: I am deprived of the residue of my years.

11   I said, I shall not see the Lord, even the Lord, in the land of the living: I shall behold man no more with the inhabitants of the world.

12   Mine age is departed, and is removed from me as a shepherd's tent: I have cut off like a weaver my life: he will cut me off with pining sickness: from day even to night wilt thou make an end of me.

13   I reckoned till morning, that, as a lion, so will he break all my bones: from day even to night wilt thou make an end of me.

14   Like a crane or a swallow, so did I chatter: I did mourn as a dove: mine eyes fail with looking upward: O Lord, I am oppressed; undertake for me.

15   What shall I say? he heath both spoken unto me, and himself hath done it: I shall go softly all my years in the bitterness of my soul.

16   O Lord, by these things men live, and in all these things is the life of my spirit: so wilt thou recover me, and make me to live.

17   Behold, for peace I had great bitterness: but thou hast in love to my soul delivered it from the pit of corruption: for thou hast cast all my sins behind thy back.

18   For the grave cannot praise thee, death can not celebrate thee: they that go down into the pit cannot hope for thy truth.

19   The living, the living, he shall praise thee, as I do this day: the father to the children shall make known thy truth.

20   The Lord was ready to save me: therefore we will sing my songs to the stringed instruments all the days of our life in the house of the Lord.

Canticle

Luke 1:14 - And thou shalt have joy and gladness; and many shall rejoice at his birth.

15   For he shall be great in the sight of the Lord, and shall drink neither wine nor strong drink; and he shall be filled with the Holy Ghost, even from his mother's womb.

16   And many of the children of Israel shall he turn to the Lord their God.

17   And he shall go before him in the spirit and power of Elias, to turn the hearts of the fathers to the children, and the disobedient to the wisdom of the just; to make ready a people prepared for the Lord.

Magnificat

Luke 1:46 - And Mary said, My soul doth magnify the Lord,

47   And my spirit hath rejoiced in God my Saviour.

48   For he hath regarded the low estate of his handmaiden: for, behold, from henceforth all generations shall call me blessed.

49   For he that is mighty hath done to me great things; and holy is his name.

50   And his mercy is on them that fear him from generation to generation.

51   He hath shewed strength with his arm; he hath scattered the proud in the imagination of their hearts.

52   He hath put down the mighty from their seats, and exalted them of low degree.

53   He hath filled the hungry with good things; and the rich he hath sent empty away.

54   He hath holpen his servant Israel, in remembrance of his mercy;

55   As he spake to our fathers, to Abraham, and to his seed for ever.

Benedictus

Luke 1:67 - And his father Zacharias was filled with the Holy Ghost, and prophesied, saying,

68   Blessed be the Lord God of Israel; for he hath visited and redeemed his people,

69   And hath raised up an horn of salvation for us in the house of his servant David;

70   As he spake by the mouth of his holy prophets, which have been since the world began;

71   That we should be saved from our enemies, and from the hand of all that hate us;

72   To perform the mercy promised to our fathers, and to remember his holy covenant;

73   The oath which he sware to our father Abraham,

74   that he would grant unto us, that we being delivered out of the hand of our enemies might serve him without fear.

75   In holiness and righteousness before him, all the days of our life.

76   And thou, child, shalt be called the prophet of the Highest: for thou shalt go before the face of the Lord to prepare his ways;

77   To give knowledge of salvation unto his people by the remission of their sins.

78   Through the tender mercy of our God; whereby the dayspring from on high hath visited us,

79   To give light to them that sit in darkness and in the shadow of death, to guide our feet into the way of peace.

From the Book of Luke

Luke 2:29 - Lord, now lettest thou thy servant depart in peace, according to thy word:

30   For mine eyes have seen thy salvation,

31   Which thou hast prepared before the face of all people;

32   A light to lighten the Gentiles, and the glory of thy people Israel.

Two Excerpts from the Book of Revelation

Revelation 5:9 - And they sung a new song, saying, Thou art worthy to take the book, and to open the seals thereof: for thou wast slain, and hast redeemed us to God by thy blood out of every kindred, and tongue, and people, and nation;

10   And hast made us unto our God kings and priests: and we shall reign on the earth.

Revelation 15:3 - And they sing the song of Moses the servant of God, and the song of the Lamb, saying, Great and marvellous are thy works, Lord God Almighty; just and true are thy ways, thou King of saints.

4   Who shall not fear thee, O Lord, and glorify thy name? for thou only art holy: for all nations shall come and worship before thee; for thy judgments are made manifest.

The Song of Solomon

The Biblical book entitled "Song of Solomon" is non-religious in nature, containing approximately twenty-five lyric poems about courtship, perhaps intended to be sung at weddings.

1:1 - The song of songs, which is Solomon's.

2   Let him kiss me with the kisses of his mouth: for thy love is better than wine.

3   Because of the savour of thy good ointments thy name is as ointment poured forth, therefore do the virgins love thee.

4   Draw me, we will run after thee: the king hath brought me into his chambers: we will be glad and rejoice in thee, we will remember thy love more than wine: the upright love thee.

5   I am black, but comely, O ye daughters of Jerusalem, as the tents of Kedar, as the curtains of Solomon.

6   Look not upon me, because I am black, because the sun hath looked upon me: my mother's children were angry with me; they made me the keeper of the vineyards; but mine own vineyard have I not kept.

7   Tell me, O thou whom my soul loveth, where thou feedest, where thou makest thy flock to rest at noon: for why should I be as one that turneth aside by the flocks of thy companions?

8   If thou know not, O thou fairest among women, go thy way forth by the footsteps of the flock, and feed thy kids beside the shepherds' tents.

9   I have compared thee, O my love, to a company of horses in Pharaoh's chariots.

10   Thy cheeks are comely with rows of jewels, thy neck with chains of gold.

11   We will make thee borders of gold with studs of silver.

12   While the king sitteth at his table, my spikenard sendeth forth the smell thereof.

13   A bundle of myrrh is my wellbeloved unto me; he shall lie all night betwixt my breasts.

14   My beloved is unto me as a cluster of camphire in the vineyards of Engedi.

15   Behold, thou art fair, my love; behold, thou art fair; thou hast doves' eyes.

16   Behold, thou art fair, my beloved, yea, pleasant: also our bed is green.

17   The beams of our house are cedar, and our rafters of fir.

2:1 - I am the rose of Sharon, and the lily of the valleys.

2   As the lily among thorns, so is my love among the daughters.

3   As the apple tree among the trees of the wood, so is my beloved among the sons. I sat down under his shadow with great delight, and his fruit was sweet to my taste.

4   He brought me to the banqueting house, and his banner over me was love.

5   Stay me with flagons, comfort me with apples: for I am sick of love.

6   His left hand is under my head, and his right hand doth embrace me.

7   I charge you, O ye daughters of Jerusalem, by the roes, and by the hinds of the field, that ye stir not up, nor awake my love, till he please.

8   The voice of my beloved! behold, he cometh leaping upon the mountains, skipping upon the hills.

9   My beloved is like a roe or a young hart: behold, he standeth behind our wall, he looketh forth at the windows, shewing himself through the lattice.

10   My beloved spake, and said unto me, Rise up, my love, my fair one, and come away.

11   For, lo, the winter is past, the rain is over and gone;

12   The flowers appear on the earth; the time of the singing of birds is come, and the voice of the turtle is heard in our land;

13   The fig tree putteth forth her greenfigs, and the vines with the tender grape give a good smell. Arise, my love, my fair one, and come away.

14   O my dove, that art in the clefts of the rock, in the secret places of the stairs, let me see thy countenance, let me hear thy voice; for sweet is thy voice, and thy countenance is comely.

15   Take us the foxes, the little foxes, that spoil the vines: for our vines have tender grapes.

16   My beloved is mine, and I am his: he feedeth among the liles.

17   Until the day break, and the shadows flee away, turn, my beloved, and be thou like a roe or a young hart upon the mountains of Bether.

3:1 - By night on my bed I sought him whom my soul loveth: I sought him, but I found him not.

2   I will rise now, and go about the city in the streets, and in the broad ways I will seek him whom my soul loveth: I sought him, but I found him not.

3   The watchmen that go about the city found me: to whom I said, Saw ye him whom my soul loveth?

4   It was but a little that I passed from them, but I found him whom my soul loveth: I held him, and would not let him go, until I had brought him into my mother's house, and into the chamber of her that conceived me.

5   I charge you, O ye daughters of Jerusalem, by the roes, and by the hinds of the field, that ye stir not up, nor awake my love, till he please.

6   Who is this that cometh out of the wilderness like pillars of smoke, perfumed with myrrh and frankincense, with all powders of the merchant?

7   Behold his bed, whish is Solomon's; three score valiant men are about it, of the valiant of Israel.

8   They all hold swords, being expert in war: every man hath his sword upon his thigh because of fear in the night.

9   King Solomon made himself a chariot of the wood of Lebanon.

10   He made the pillars thereof of silver, the bottom thereof of gold, the covering of it of purple, the midst thereof being paved with love, for the daughters of Jerusalem.

11   Go forth, O ye daughters of Zion, and behold king Solomon with the crown wherewith his mother crowned him in the day of his espousals, and in the day of the gladness of his heart.

4:1 -   Behold, thou art fair, my love; behold, thou art fair; thou hast doves' eyes within thy locks: thy hair is as a flock of goats, that appear from mount Gilead.

2   Thy teeth are like a flock of sheep that are even shorn, which came up from the washing; whereof every one bear twins, and none is barren among them.

3   Thy lips are like a thread of scarlet, and thy speech is comely: thy temples are like a piece of a pomegranate within thy locks.

4   Thy neck is like the tower of David builded for an armoury, whereon there hang a thousand bucklers, all shields of mighty men.

5   Thy two breasts are like two young roes that are twins, which feed among the lilies.

6   Until the day break, and the shadows flee away, I will get me to the mountain of myrrh, and to the hill of frankincense.

7   Thou art all fair, my love; there is no spot in thee.

8   Come with me from Lebanon, my spouse, with me from Lebanon: look from the top of Amana, from the top of Shenir and Hermon, from the lions' dens, from the mountains of the leopards.

9   Thou hast raised my heart, my sister, my spouse; thou hast ravished my heart with one of thine eyes, with one chain of thy neck.

10   How fair is thy love, my sister, my spouse! how much better is thy love than wine! and the smell of thine ointments than all spices!

11   Thy lips, O my spouse, drop as the honeycomb: honey and milk are under thy tongue; and the smell of thy garments is like the smell of Lebanon.

12   A garden inclosed is my sister, my spouse; a spring shut up, a fountain sealed.

13   Thy plants are an orchard of pomegranates, with pleasant fruits; camphire, with spikenard,

14   Spikenard and saffron; calamus and cinnamon, with all trees of frankincense; myrrh and aloes, with all the chief spices:

15   A fountain of gardens, a well of living waters, and streams from Lebanon.

16   Awake, O north wind; and come, thou south; blow upon my garden, that the spices thereof may flow out. Let my beloved come into this garden, and eat his pleasant fruits.

5:1 - I am come into my garden, my sister, my spouse; I have gathered my myrrh with my spice; I have eaten my honeycomb with my hone; I have drunk my wine with my milk: eat, O friends; drink, yea, drink abundantly, O beloved.

2   I sleep, but my heart waketh: it is the voice of my beloved that knocketh, saying, Open to me, my sister, my love, my dove, my undefiled: for my head is filled with dew, and my locks with the drops of the night.

3   I have put off my coat; how shall I put it on? I have washed my feet; how shall I defile them?

4   My beloved put in his hand by the hole of the door, and my bowels were moved for him.

5   I rose up to open to my beloved; and my hands dropped with myrrh, and my fingers with sweet smelling myrrh, upon the handles of the lock.

6   I opened to my beloved; but my beloved had withdrawn himself, and was gone: my soul failed when he spake: I sought him, but I could not find him; I called him, but he gave me no answer.

7   The watchmen that went about the city found me, they smote me, they wounded me; the keepers of the walls took away my veil from me.

8   I charge you, O daughters of Jerusalem, if ye find my beloved, that ye tell him, that I am sick of love.

9   What is thy beloved more than another beloved, O thou fairest among women? what is thy beloved more than another beloved, that thou dost so charge us?

10   My beloved is white and ruddy, the chiefest among ten thousand.

11   His head is as the most fine gold, his locks are bushy, and black as a raven.

12   His eyes are as the eyes of doves by the rivers of waters, washed with milk, and fitly set.

13   His cheeks are as a bed of spices, as sweet flowers: his lips like lilies, dropping sweet smelling myrrh.

14   His hands are as gold rings set with the beryl: his belly is as bright ivory overlaid with sapphires.

15   His legs are as pillars of marble, set upon sockets of fine gold: his countenance is as Lebanon, excellent as the cedars.

16   His mouth is most sweet: yea, he is altogether lovely. This is my beloved, and this is my friend, O daughters of Jerusalem.

6:1 - Whither is thy beloved gone, O thou fairest among women? whither is thy beloved turned aside: that we may seek him with thee.

2   My beloved is gone down into his garden, to the beds of spices, to feed in the gardens, and to gather lilies.

3   I am my beloved's, and my beloved is mine: he feedeth among the lilies.

4   Thou art beautiful, O my love, as Tirzah, comely as Jerusalem, terrible as an army with banners.

5   Turn away thine eyes from me, for they have overcome me: thy hair is as a flock of goats that appear from Gilead.

6   Thy teeth are as a flock of sheep which go up from the washing, whereof every one beareth twins, and there is not one barren among them.

7   As a piece of pomegranate are thy temples within thy locks.

8   There are threescore queens, and fourscore concubines, and virgins without number.

9   My dove, my undefiled is but one; she is the only one of her mother, she is the choice one of her that bare her. The daughters saw her, and blessed her; yea, the queens and the concubines, and they praised her.

10   Who is she that looketh forth as the morning, fair as the moon, clear as the sun, and terrible as an army with banners?

11   I went down into the garden of nuts to see the fruits of the valley, and to see whether the vine flourished, and the pomegranates budded.

12   Or ever I was aware, my soul made me like the chariots of Amminadib.

13   Return, return, O Shulamite; return, return, that we may look upon thee. What will ye see in the Shulamite? As it were the company of two armies.

7:1 - How beautiful are thy feet with shoes, O prince's daughter! the joints of thy thighs are like jewels, the work of the hands of a cunning workman.

2   Thy navel is like a round goblet, which wanteth not liquor: thy belly is like an heap of wheat set about with lilies.

3   Thy two breasts are like two young roes that are twins.

4   Thy neck is as a tower of ivory; thine eyes like the fishpools in Heshbon, by the gate of Bathrabbim: thy nose is as the tower of Lebanon which looketh toward Damascus.

5   Thine head upon thee is like Carmel, and the hair of thine head like purple; the king is held in the galleries.

6   How fair and how pleasant art thou. O love, for delights!

7   This thy stature is like to a palm tree, and thy breasts to clusters of grapes.

8   I said, I will go up to the palm tree, I will take hold of the boughs thereof: now also thy breasts shall be as clusters of the vine, and the smell of thy nose like apples;

9   And the roof of thy mouth like the best wine for my beloved, that goeth down sweetly, causing the lips of those that are asleep to speak.

10   I am my beloved's, and his desire is toward me.

11   Come, my beloved, let us go forth into the field; let us lodge in the villages.

12   Let us get up early to the vineyards; let us see if the vine flourish, whether the tender grape appear, and the pomegranates bud forth: there will I give thee my loves.

13   The mandrakes give a smell, and at our gates are all manner of pleasant fruits, new and old, which I have laid up for thee, O my beloved.

8:1 - O that thou were as my brother, that sucked the breasts of my mother! when I should find thee without, I would kiss thee; yea, I should not be despised.

2   I would lead thee, and bring thee into my mother's house, who would instruct me: I would cause thee to drink of spiced wine of the juice of my pomegranate.

3   His left hand should be under my head, and his right hand should embrace me.

4   I charge you, O daughters of Jerusalem, that ye stir not up, nor awake my love, until he please.

5   Who is this that cometh up from the wilderness, leaning upon her beloved? I raised thee up under the apple tree: there thy mother brought thee forth: there she brought thee forth that bare thee.

6   Set me as a seal upon thine heart, as a seal upon thine arm: for love is strong as death; jealousy is cruel as the grave: the coals thereof are coals of fire, which hath a most vehement flame.

7   Many waters cannot quench love, neither can the floods drown it: if a man would give all the substance of his house for love, it would utterly be contemned.

8   We have a little sister, and she hath no breasts: what shall we do for our sister in the day when she shall be spoken for?

146

9   If she be a wall, we will build upon her a palace of silver: and if she be a door, we will inclose her with boards of cedar.

10   I am a wall, and my breasts like towers: then was I in his eyes as one that found favour.

11   Solomon had a vineyard at Baalhamon; he let out the vineyard unto keepers; every one for the fruit thereof was to bring a thousand pieces of silver.

12   My vineyard, which is mine, is before me: thou, O Solomon, must have a thousand, and those that keep the fruit thereof two hundred.

13   Thou that dwellest in the gardens, the companions hearken to they voice: cause me to hear it.

14   Make haste, my beloved, and be thou like to a roe or to a young hart upon the mountains of spices.

AFTERWORD

The entire Biblical book of Psalms could be included in this volume, but has been left out. The Psalms in their original version were songs, perhaps with instrumental accompaniment. The indication "selah" that appears variously throughout the Psalms might have been a liturgical direction regarding performance in a service. It might have indicated an instrumental interlude, for example. The various headings that precede many of the Psalms, like "To the chief Musician upon Gittith," may have been codes denoting certain melody types.

Collections of Psalms in the past five hundred years have been called psalters, perhaps dating from the 3rd Century A.D. Although different translations of the Psalms produce various rhythms and meters in musical notation, the Psalm texts can best be described as poetic in nature, or perhaps as "poetic prose." Often a given section within a Psalm is reflected or amplified verbally and ideologically in a following section. This characteristic led to types of performance in the early church in which a soloist and choir, or two small choirs, would alternate sections of the Psalms: these types of performance are known as responsorial and antiphonal psalmody, and are present in the late 20th Century during Psalm singing.

Presumably the present volume of musical references and song texts in the Holy Bible, supplemented with the Biblical book of Psalms, will present the reader with plenty of food for musical thought.

BIBLIOGRAPHY

Dictionaries and Encyclopedias

Adato, Joseph and Judy, George. The Percussionist's Dictionary. Melville, New York: Belwin-Mills, 1984.

Apel, Willi. Harvard Dictionary of Music, second edition. Cambridge, Massachusetts: Harvard University Press, 1969.

Harris, William H. and Levey, Judith S. The New Columbia Encyclopedia. New York and London: Columbia University Press, 1975.

Bibles

Good News Bible. New York: American Bible Society, 1966.

Holy Bible, Authorized King James Version. Iowa Falls, Iowa: World Bible Publishers.

Jerusalem Bible, The. Garden City, New York: Doubleday and Company, 1966.

New English Bible, The. England and U.S.A.: Oxford University Press, Cambridge University Press, 1970.

Revised Standard Version Bible. U.S.A.: Division of Christian Education of the National Council of the Churches of Christ, 1971.

Books

Blades, James. Percussion Instruments and Their History, revised edition. London: Faber and Faber, 1984.

Cannon, Johnson, Waite. The Art of Music. New York: Harper and Row, 1960.

Crocker, Richard L. A History of Musical Style. New York: McGraw-Hill, 1966.

Fang, C. N. Bishop's Message 1976-1988. Kuala Lumpur and Penang, Malaysia: Board of Christian Education, Chinese Annual Conference of the Methodist Church, 1988.

Flannery, Austin P., editor. Documents of Vatican II. Grand Rapids, Michigan: William B. Eerdsmans, 1978.

Grout, Donald J. A History of Western Music, third edition. New York: W. W. Norton, 1980.

Marcuse, Sibyl. A Survey of Musical Instruments. New York: Harper and Row, 1975.

Montagu, Jeremy. The World of Medieval and Renaissance Musical Instruments. Woodstock, New York: Overlook Press, 1976.

Peters, Gordon B. The Drummer: Man, revised edition. Wilmette, Illinois: Kemper-Peters, 1975.

Putnam, Nathanael D. Musical Instruments in Biblical Times. Fullerton, California: F. E. Olds and Son, 1967.

Sachs, Curt. The History of Musical Instruments. New York: W. W. Norton, 1940.

Articles

Greene, David M. "Dictional Intelligibility." Musical Heritage Review 12/16 (1988), 12.

Greene, David M. "Exquisite." Musical Heritage Review 13/1 (1989), 3.

Larrick, Geary. "Percussion and the Beauty of Celebration." News Notes 33/5 (March 1988), 11-12.

Larrick, Geary. "Percussion: Its Status from Antiquity to the Modern Era." Percussionist VI/2 (December 1968), 42-49.

Newsletters of the Ethnic Minority Local Church Development Committee. Sun Prairie, Wisconsin: Wisconsin Conference of the United Methodist Church, 1986-1988.

Saliers, Don E. "On Singing and Praying the Psalms." News Notes 34/5 (February-March 1989), 7.

Recordings

Faure, Gabriel. "Requiem, Op. 48." Philharmonic Orchestra and Ambrosian Singers with soloists. New York: CBS-Odyssey YT 39787, 1985.

Foss, Lukas. Ives, Charles. Stravinsky, Igor. "Psalms." "Psalm 67." "Symphony of Psalms." Milwaukee Symphony Orchestra and Wisconsin Conservatory Symphony Chorus. Minneapolis, Minnesota: Pro Arte, PCD-169, 1984.

150

"Gregorian Chants." Monks of the Benedictine Abbey and the Boys' Choir
from L'Alumnat. Century City, California: Everest 3346.

Handel, George Frederick. "Messiah." Philadelphia Orchestra and
Mormon Tabernacle Choir with soloists. U.S.A.: Columbia M2L-
263, ML 5405-6.

Music

Book of Hymns, The. Nashville, Tennessee: United Methodist Publishing
House, 1966.

Larrick, Geary. "Exclamation!" Sermon by Martin Luther King, Jr. with
incidental music. Stevens Point, Wisconsin: G and L Publishing,
1989.

Moore, James L. "Psalm Collage." Columbus, Ohio: Permus Publications,
1978.

United Methodist Hymnal, The. Nashville, Tennessee: United Methodist
Publishing House, 1989.

INDEX

African, 32
America, 1, 19
analysis, 29, 36
aria, 98, 113
Asia, 13, 44
audience, 22

Bach, J.S., 48
bagpipe, 2
ballet, 22
bamboo, 19
Baroque, 19, 31
behavior, 109
Boehm, Theobold, 19

China, 13, 17
cimbalom, 17
civilization, 3, 32
clapper, 9
clay, 19
composer, 112
congregation, 29
connoisseur, 13

dancing, 2, 43
Debussy, Claude, 13
deviations, 3
drum, 1, 6, 50, 92, 95

educator, 5
emotions, 31
England, 1, 5, 10, 19
ethnomusicology, 3
ethos, 44
Europe, 1, 9, 17, 19, 50, 59, 91, 95, 98, 109

Far East, 1
fellowship, 4
fife, 1, 19
form, 31, 36, 38, 113

German, 19
glockenspiel, 9
gong, 2
Greece, 6, 22, 29
Greek, 1, 44, 112

Handel, G.F., 19, 98

harmony, 29, 38, 44
harpsichord, 17, 59
Heaven, 22
Hebrew, 1, 82, 112
horn, 2, 63, 98
hymnology, 29

India, 9
Indian, 19, 32
Indonesia, 13

Japan, 13
Japanese, 9, 32
jazz, 44
Jewish, 63
Jews, 22
jingles, 6, 95

keyboard, 5, 6, 17, 22, 48
kithara, 22

Latin, 1
lute, 1
lyre, 1, 2, 22
lyric, 112

mallet, 9, 13, 17, 59
Mendelssohn, Felix, 82
Mesopotamia, 22
meter, 112, 147
middle ages, 22, 50
Middle East, 13
minstrels, 3
mouthpiece, 10, 98

natural science, 29
North America, 9, 17, 89
opera, 113
oratorio, 98, 113
orchestra, 9, 10, 19, 22, 23, 65, 98

palette, 13
pantaleon, 17
percussion, 5, 6, 9, 13, 31, 92, 95
personality, 44
photograph, 3, 36
piano, 5, 9, 82
pianoforte, 17, 59
piccolo, 19
pitch, 9, 10, 13, 19, 22, 36, 59, 65
plastic, 19
plectrum, 6

poetry, 112, 147
printing, 1
psalmody, 147
psalter, 52, 147

Ravel, Maurice, 22
recitative, 98, 113
recorder, 19
Renaissance, 10, 19, 22, 92, 95
rhyme, 112
rhythm, 36, 38, 75, 95, 112, 147

science, 44
Shakespearean dialect, 5
shofar, 63
soul, 44, 75, 113
soundboard, 59
soundbox, 36
syntax, 112

tabor, 50, 92
tambourine, 2, 6, 95
Tchaikovsky, Peter, 13, 22
Telemann, G.P., 19
tom-tom, 50, 92
trombone, 65

United States, 10, 19

valves, 10, 98
violin, 23, 109
voice, 5, 66, 75, 98

wind bands, 10, 19, 65

xylophone, 6

zither, 2, 3, 4, 17

STUDIES IN THE HISTORY
AND INTERPRETATION OF MUSIC

1. Hugo Meynell, **The Art of Handel's Operas**

2. Dale Jorgenson, **Moritz Hauptmann of Leipzig**

3. Nancy van Deusen (ed.), **The Harp and The Soul: Essays in Medieval Music**

4. James L. Taggert, **Franz Joseph Haydn's Keyboard Sonatas: An Untapped Gold Mine**

5. William E. Grim, **The Faust Legend in Music and Literature**

6. Richard L. LaCroix, **Augustine on Music: An Interdisciplinary Collection of Essays**

7. Clifford Taylor, **Musical Idea and Design Aesthetic in Contemporary Music: A Text for Discerning Appraisal of Musical Thought in Western Culture**

8. Mary Gilbertson, **The Metaphysics of Alliteration in** *Pearl*

9. Geary Larrick, **Musical References and Song Texts in the Bible**

10. Felix-Eberhard von Cube, **The Book of the Musical Artwork: An Interpretation of the Musical Theories of Heinrich Schenker,** David Neumeyer, George Boyd and Scott Harris (trans.)

11. Robert Luoma, **Music, Mode, and Words in Orlando Di Lasso's Last Works**

12. John A. Kimmey Jr., **A Critique of Musicology: Clarifying the Scope, Limits, and Purposes of Musicology**

13. Kent Holliday, **Reproducing Pianos Past and Present**

14. Gloria Shafer, **Origins of the Children's Song Cycle as a Genre with Four Case Studies and an Original Song Cycle**

15. Bertil van Boer, **Dramatic Cohesion in the Music of Joseph Martin Kraus: From Sacred Music to Symphonic Form**

16. William O. Cord, **The Teutonic Mythology of Richard Wagner's** *The Ring of The Nibelung,* **Volume One: Nine Dramatic Properties**

17. William O. Cord, **The Teutonic Mythology of Richard Wagner's** *The Ring of The Nibelung,* **Volume Two: The Family of Gods**

18. William O. Cord, **The Teutonic Mythology of Richard Wagner's** *The Ring of The Nibelung,* **Volume Three: The Natural and Supernatural Worlds**

19. Victorien Sardou, *LA TOSCA* (**The Drama Behind the Opera**), W. Laird Kleine-Ahlbrandt (trans.)

20. Herbert W. Richardson (ed.), **New Studies in Richard Wagner's** *The Ring of The Nibelung*

21. Catherine Dower, **Yella Pessl, First Lady of the Harpsichord**

22. Margaret Scheppach, **Dramatic Parallels in Michael Tippett's Opera: Analytical Essays on the Musico-Dramatic Techniques**

23. William E. Grim, **Haydn's** *"Sturm Und Drang"* **Symphonies: Form and Meaning**

24. Klemens Diez, **Constanze, Formerly Widow of Mozart: Her Unwritten Memoir Based on Historical Documents**, Joseph Malloy (trans.)

25. Harold E. Fiske, **Music and Mind: Philosophical Essays on the Cognition and Meaning of Music**

26. Anne Trenkamp and John G. Suess, **Studies in the Schoenbergian Movement in Vienna and the United States:** *Essays in Honor of Marcel Dick*

27. Harvey Stokes, **A Selected Annotated Bibliography on Italian Serial Composers**

28. Julia Muller, **Words and Music in Henry Purcell's First Semi-Opera,** *Dioclesian:* **An Approach to Early Music Through Early Theatre**

29. Ronald W. Holz, **Eric Leidzen: Band Arranger and Composer**

30. Enrique Moreno, **Expanded Tunings in Contemporary Music: Theoretical Innovations and Practical Applications**

31. Charles H. Parsons, (compiler), **A Benjamin Britten Discography**

32. Denis Wilde, **The Development of Melody in the Tone Poems of Richard Strauss: Motif, Figure, and Theme**